21542

I100E563

The Holy Spirit

the Holy Spirit

Eduard Schweizer

translated by
REGINALD H. and ILSE FULLER

FORTRESS PRESS   Philadelphia

Library of Congress Cataloging in Publication Data

Schweizer, Eduard, 1913–
  The Holy Spirit.

  Translation of Heiliger Geist.
  Includes bibliographical references.
  1. Holy Spirit. I. Title.
BT121.2.S3813   231'.3   79-8892
ISBN 0-8006-0629-9

8009E80 Printed in the United States of America 1-629

Contents

1

What Is
the Holy Spirit?

Views of the Spirit in the
Western World

As recently as the seventeenth century it was quite possible to sing without inhibition, in devotion and joy of the Holy Spirit:

Lead us, Holy Spirit, in holiness
Throughout our whole life long
That we may know the worthlessness
Of carnal lusts so strong.[1]

Does this mean that the Spirit is the opposite of whatever is bodily, natural, and physical—and especially sexual—in short, the opposite of "carnal lusts"? That is roughly the way people thought even in the eighteenth century as they looked for an escape from the trammels of everyday life where toil and sweat and suffering were their lot. They sought to rise to the higher levels of the spirit, to an ideal world where they could discuss all that was beautiful and good—provided of course, they had sufficient wealth and leisure to do so.

By contrast, at the turn of the nineteenth century Hegel saw the Spirit of God primarily in the great movements of history. Finally, following in Hegel's footsteps, Karl Marx protested against this idealizing of a "spiritual" world which was higher and divine. Marx championed the rights of all who lived and worked on this earth, thus emphasizing the historic significance of the economic and material order. This mistrust of a spirit which shuns the material world as much as possible is still influential in Marxist circles today. Perhaps the skeptic was right after all when, back in the days of the stage coach, he declared that he could get along all right with God the Father and Creator, and even with Jesus the Son, but that when it came to the Holy Ghost he felt as if he were dealing with a third horse, the extra held in reserve: you always had to pay to keep it ready even though you never actually saw it and it probably did not exist at all.

If however, we leave the Western world and consider Africa instead, we find that there are people for whom the idea of the Holy Spirit seems the most natural thing in the world: In his Spirit God lives in the hearts of men and women, moving and inspiring them, calling them to action or granting them peace and quietness. Where else but in his Spirit could God's presence be experienced? That is the way people think who still have a direct relation to God.

The Church's Ministry as the Locus of the Holy Spirit

The question as to where the Holy Spirit was speaking and where he was not came up even in the earliest Christian community. Paul emphasized that a primary criterion for the working of the Spirit was whether Jesus was acknowledged as Lord and the community was built up (1 Cor. 12:3, 7; 14:1-5). For John, the criterion was whether people acknowledged "Christ come in the flesh," Christ meaning Jesus and all he did on earth (1 John 4:1-6). According to Matthew 7:21-23 what matters is whether a person who is moved by the Spirit lives his whole life according to God's will.

That raised great problems quite early on. At any rate, a Church Order deriving perhaps from Syria at the end of the first century laid it down that any wandering prophet who accepts the hospitality of a local church for more than two days, who is moved by the Spirit to ask for a meal or, worse still, begs for money, is a false prophet and should be sent packing (*Did.* 11:5-6, 9). It is a real problem how to distinguish between the genuine and false prophets, and we can understand how the early church wanted assurances on the subject.

Thus at the end of the second century we read in Irenaeus that the bishops received the charisma of truth[2] when they entered into the unbroken line of episcopal succession. In this way it was possible to distinguish where the Holy Spirit spoke and where he did not. In the third century a doctor of theology in Rome, who was for some time a bishop, taught that the knowledge of God depended upon the "Holy Ghost transmitted in the church, first received by the apostles and by them imparted to such as were of orthodox belief. . . . Their successors were participators in this grace, the high priesthood and the office of teaching, and therefore were acknowledged as guardians of the church."[3]

At the Council of Trent, where the Roman Catholic Church distanced itself from the Reformation, it is affirmed that "by sacred ordination the Holy Ghost is imparted." Thus "the bishops who have succeeded the apostles . . . have been placed by the Holy Ghost to rule the Church of God" and "if anyone says that by sacred ordination the Holy Ghost is not imparted . . . let him be anathema."[4]

Does this mean that the Holy Spirit is guaranteed as the exclusive possession of the clergy? Are they alone to decide whether or not the laity have the genuine and true Spirit of God?

The Bible as the Locus of the Holy Spirit

The Reformers too were looking for a guarantee of the presence of the Holy Spirit. They too needed to know where the Holy Spirit was present and where he was not. They thought they could find their guarantee in the Bible. The Augsburg Confession, which the Lutherans presented in 1530 before the Emperor and the Diet, seeking to emphasize their unity with the Roman Catholic Church, asserts that the Holy Spirit is imparted through word and sacrament as by instruments (AC, Art. 5). This ties the Spirit's operation to the church's services. Calvin (1509–1564) added the "secret" or "internal witness" of the Holy Spirit, through which "the same Spirit, who spake by the mouths of the prophets, should penetrate into our hearts" in order to convince us of the true tradition of the Word of God.[5] In the Second Helvetic Confession (1562) the Reformed Church adopted Calvin's concern and emphasized the role of the Holy Spirit which "by means of the preaching of the gospel and the prayer of faith [ET "steadfast prayer"] and in the receiving of the sacrament conveys 'invisibly' and 'inwardly in the soul' what the word or sacrament is intended to give us."[6]

But soon stricter rules were made. Quite early Ursinus (1534-83) expressed the opinion that God "illumines and rules the thoughts (of the biblical authors), so as to prevent them from error in any matter of doctrine" and Cocceius (1603-69) put it this way: "As they spoke not by their own will, but impelled by the Holy Ghost, so did they write."

Then Voetius (1589-1676) asserted categorically that Holy Scripture is true and reliable in matters of history: ". . . *truth free from error and inspired by God,* permeating each and every single part thereof, so that its authors brought forth each and every sentence both in content and in form not according to their own impulse and ideas, but by the dictation of the Holy Ghost," and that includes even the vowel pointing of the consonantal Hebrew text in the Old Testament. This becomes the universal standard by which truth and error are measured. As Ursinus puts it, "We acknowledge as judge, not the church but the Holy Ghost, who speaks to us in Holy Scripture and gives his word in a way in which we may clearly perceive it." Hence any other kind of faith, or worse unbelief, can only be taken as an act against the conscience, an act of resistance against the Holy Spirit. We see again in Heidegger (1633-98) where the battle lines are drawn—against "the enthusiasts, who wish to sell an irrational excitement of the heart for one that is of God."[7] Similar statements are found in Lutheran theologians of that time.

Does this mean that the Holy Spirit is available only in a "preserved" condition, in the centuries-old formulations of the Bible? Or at least: Is the Spirit guaranteed there in such a way that not a letter or a vowel point is in error? Is the Spirit, so to speak, encapsulated within the Bible, and do all his pronouncements have to measure up to what the Bible says?

The Human Heart as the Locus
of the Holy Spirit

On the Catholic side, then, the guarantee was sought in the magisterium; on the Protestant side, in the Bible. Both sides wanted to have the Holy Spirit under human control. In one case the guarantee was ordination to the church's ministry; in the other, a minister's expertise in expounding the Scripture.

But there is also a diametrically opposite thread running all through the history of the church. In an early Church Order we hear of wandering prophets who speak in tongues under the impulse of the Spirit; they must never be criticized or interrupted—to do so would be to commit the unforgivable sin against the Holy Ghost. In the mid-second century there appeared in Asia Minor a man named Montanus who believed he was the embodiment of the Holy Spirit which Jesus had promised. He had a following of prophets and especially of prophetesses who spoke in ecstasy and announced the impending end of the world and descent of the heavenly Jerusalem. They followed a strict rule of life which required fasting. They regarded mortal sins as unforgivable. They prohibited second marriages, and would not countenance flight in times of persecution. Such were the characteristics of this movement. It soon spread to Italy, Gaul, and North Africa.[8] In the third century we hear of men and women living together in strict sexual abstinence. They went about the country singly or in groups, visiting the faithful, expelling demons, calling the brethren together, and in reliance solely on the Holy Ghost—without any training in public speaking—preaching the gospel.[9] Some new evidence about a similar group in roughly the same period has recently turned up. They called themselves "the Little Ones" and avoided all those who attached importance to worldly goods or desired earthly creatures. They even refused to have anything to do with the church because its bishops and deacons demanded places of honor. They personally received a plenary inspiration of the Holy Spirit which enabled them to see what no one else could see, and hear what only celestial beings could hear.[10]

In the twelfth century Joachim of Fiore caused great excitement throughout the church by teaching that following the Old Testament age of the Father and the New Testament age of the Son, the monastic age of the Spirit was dawning and with it the turning point of the ages. [11] Thomas Müntzer (1468?-1525) studied his writings and, under the influence of the prophets at Zwickau, came to believe that inner illumination was more important than the Bible, and personal experience of the cross more important than the doctrine of justification. He believed he was the incarnation of John the Baptist, whose mission it was to prepare the reign of Christ. Müntzer hoped to establish a theocracy where "tyrants and churchly-faced persons are to be strangled."[12]

At the time of the Reformation the city of Münster saw the appearance of Jan Matthys and Jan Beuckelsson who tried to establish the kingdom of God right there in Münster. They abolished Sundays and Holy Days and held agape meals in the Cathedral Square. They executed unpopular citizens, introduced polygamy and the common ownership of property, and burned documents and books wholesale — everything except the Bible.[13] Less spectacular was Valentine Weigels (1533-88), who set great store by "the Book of the Word in our hearts," "Christ in us" as a way of knowing "from the inside out rather than from the outside in"; Weigels would have nothing to do with "steeple houses."[14] Jacob Böhme, who had been a cobbler near Görlitz since 1599, laid great stress on being born again inwardly by the Spirit; Böhme was very influential in certain circles in England.[15]

In more recent times we get the Mormons, who also trace their origins to visions inspired by the Spirit. In 1827 the prophet Joseph Smith announced the discovery of the golden tablets of Mormon which Mormon's son, the prophet Moroni, had hidden in A.D. 421. Smith claimed he had been able in a vision to translate the unknown writing and discovered it to contain the pre-history of America. After the Tower of Babel was built (Gen.11) a first party of settlers came to the North American continent; they were followed by another party in 600 B.C. At Easter the Risen Lord appeared in America as well as in Palestine and chose twelve disciples. Smith's successor introduced polygamy in 1843 following a revelation of the Spirit, but this was repealed by another revelation in 1890. Typical for the Mormons, as for other groups, is their strict rule of life. They abstain from alcohol and tobacco, and often from coffee, tea, and meat as well.[16]

But far more important are the so-called charismatic groups which have sprung up recently on every continent. In them we find the gifts of the Holy Spirit: healing of the sick through prayer, prophetic revelations, and speaking with tongues. Sometimes the members continue to take part in the life of the churches, whose other members do not possess such gifts. Sometimes they form their own churches alongside the others, but without denying the others' right to exist. But sometimes they oppose the institutional church, which they regard as dead because it does not share their experiences. Therefore it is an open question today, and one of major importance, how the various groups should relate to one another to their mutual benefit.

What Does This Mean?

What a motley collection of phenomena we find in the history of the church—some of them extremely illuminating, some highly objectionable, and all attributed to the Holy Spirit! But where is he really to be found? Can we nail him down anywhere?

Is he perhaps to be found in the episcopate or in Holy Scripture? Assuming we have received Holy Orders through the laying on of hands, or have studied Scripture and taken a theological degree, can we then control the Holy Spirit and be sure where he is and where he is not?

Or is he instead to be identified with anything that surpasses our understanding? Is he to be found in whatever bursts upon us with elemental force and compels us to tread new and unknown paths?

In the former instances—Scripture or ministry—we may be distressed at the way people seem to have taken control of God, confident that they know everything there is to know about the Holy Spirit. In the latter instance we may be equally distressed by the way divine power and human desires are so mixed up that nobody can be really sure whether it is God who is at work or just ordinary human drives, be they conscious or otherwise.

If we proceed with great care, we may perhaps discover some common denominator in all these voices, despite their extraordinary differences. The Holy Spirit is obviously present where God is upon this earth of ours and in our midst — however we may picture him in detail — which is why it is so urgent for us to search for him. That is exactly what we need, the reality of God, his presence here and now.

Theologians have constantly debated about the starting point of theology: Should we start with God and move from him to man and the problems of human life? Or should we start from the other end, with man and his experience, and from there ascend to God? Indeed the two options have been set against each other as "theology from above" vs. "theology from below." But if we take seriously the fact that God in his Holy Spirit dwells with us, working in us and influencing us, it should be easy to discover even in the midst of our own experiences the reality of that God who as our Lord and Master stands above us with all his authority and power. And if it is really God whom we encounter in our experiences, the "theology from below" which begins with our needs and desires, our troubles and concerns, will suddenly turn into a "theology from above" because in all those things it is *he* who encounters us, the One who is greater than ourselves and our little world. It ought to be possible to know him as One who in our world — *his* creation — is strange to us, and accordingly learn to hope for the future consummation of his work. As we proceed we will want to keep these four points in mind: his strangeness, his creation, our knowing, and the future consummation.

Of course, when it comes to describing experiences, we cannot help using picture language. All human experience, including our nonreligious experience, has to rely on picture language. Every experience has observable consequences. For instance, if we fall in love it will show itself in a rise in our blood pressure, a rise which is susceptible of accurate measurement, or in a trembling of the hands where the vibrations can be measured in centimeters. But such measurable data tell us nothing about what really matters. That is something we can speak of only in picture language.

Only through picture language is it possible to create a similar mood in the listener, or to remind him of something similar that he has experienced in his own life. Thus we may speak of God as One who comes "down from above," perhaps even "vertically from above" or "from heaven" and enters our lives. Yet we know full well that heaven is not a geographical place somewhere "above" the earth. But in using this metaphor we are really making the point that we have experienced in our earthly life One who is absolutely "transcendent" (and that too is a metaphor). We want to remind those who listen to us that they too have had similar experiences. Or at least we want to ask them to imagine it possible to experience a reality that is not identical with my own self and yet speaks to me, a reality that calls me, moves me, makes demands on me, or strengthens and comforts me.

Of course, when we use the word "God" we are saying much more. We are saying that this "reality" is personal, as when someone speaks to us and evokes a response of joy, thanksgiving, petition, and obedience. In this way we are saying that the best symbol for our encounter with God is an encounter between persons in which someone gives me the help that makes all the difference in the world to me.

Both these things are so urgent today: We must learn to experience in the rough and tumble of human life the reality of God in all its difference, and we must learn to have confidence in the picture language we use to embody the reality of God — knowing full well that we cannot capture him in anything like a mathematical formula.

Should we not then consult the Bible itself and find out how the authors of the Old and New Testaments experienced the Holy Spirit, and how they attempted to express their experiences in what inevitably was picture language?

2

The Witness
of the Old Testament

The Strangeness of the Spirit

THE WORD OF GOD

Israel's first experience of the working of the Spirit was of a strange power breaking into everyday life in unpredictable ways, a power that could not be clearly recognized as being good or bad, divine or demonic. The consequences of this experience are felt so strongly throughout the Old Testament that the term "Holy Spirit" is hardly ever used. It is found only in Psalm 51:11 and Isaiah 63:10-11. 1 Samuel 19:19-24 describes the experience for us. David, persecuted by Saul, visits Samuel. Samuel and his whole school of prophets were transported in a vision; they all went on raving for hours, apparently driven by the Spirit of God. Saul's messengers succumbed to the same influence of the Spirit and behaved like the others; instead of returning to Saul as they had been ordered to do, they stayed on. Three times the same thing happened and in the end, Saul set out himself to take David prisoner or kill him. But Saul too comes under the influence of the Spirit. He tears the clothes from his body, falls to the ground in a state of exhaustion, and lies there naked for a whole day and night. A very strange story that, and very much like what has happened in the most dubious and odd sects throughout the history of the church. Here, it seems, the Spirit of God is experienced in ways that exclude all rational thought and action; the person seized by the Spirit is no longer aware of what he is doing.

There is nothing exceptional about all this. As early as 1 Samuel 10:10 there is a similar story of Saul meeting a band of prophets and falling into a state of ecstasy. As Samuel puts it in his figurative language, "the spirit of God came mightily upon him" and Saul was "turned into another man" (10:6). Even more figurative and picturesque is the description in Numbers 11:25-29 of God descending in a cloud and taking some of the spirit which had already been given to Moses and putting it upon the seventy elders, with the result that they fell into an ecstasy and could not stop it. The spirit even falls upon two elders who were not with the others but had stayed behind in the camp. Then there is the vivid story of Balaam. A spirit from God came upon him and "uncovered his eyes" so that he could see into God's plans for the future (Num. 24:2-3).

This idea, that the spirit is the source of the word which man may understand as the very word of God himself, continues in the experiences of the later prophets, although in their case there is no special emphasis on the extraordinary. All the same, when Hosea calls himself a "prophet" or, which comes to the same thing, a "man of the spirit," the whole nation regards him as a madman, as someone out of his mind (Hos. 9:7). The case of Micah is different; he draws a sharp distinction between the power and spirit of God on the one hand and the peculiar and spectacular visions and oracles of the seers and soothsayers on the other (Mic. 3:5-8). Similarly we are told that the spirit of God was in Joseph (Gen. 41:38) and David (2 Sam. 23:2), speaking through them and endowing them with genuine wisdom, though without any mention of striking phenomena. In these cases the spirit of God does not exclude man's "normal," rational mental processes, or move him to do strange acts which are incomprehensible even to himself. On the contrary, what the spirit does here is to give wisdom. In the same way it is expected that the spirit will rest upon the Messiah or Servant of God (Isa. 11:2; 42:1; 61:1). The spirit of God may even be almost identified with the prophet himself (Neh. 9:30). Thus we are already faced by the question as to who is a genuine prophet, one really moved by the Spirit of God, and who is a false prophet acting on his own initiative. Israel learned that extraordinary phenomena were in themselves no guarantee of divine inspiration as distinct from human speech. Where a person loses control over himself and does not realize what he is saying, there is no guarantee that it is God speaking through him. Even the Old Testament is aware of this. But if the type and manner of the phenomenon tells us nothing one way or the other, how can we distinguish between the true prophet and the false? One sign of the difference, though a highly provisional one, can often be observed. With all of us it is our own wishes and dreams that so often come to the surface. Where the things the spirit seems to say bear a suspicious resemblance to our own wishes and dreams we are justified in being skeptical. That is why the false prophet generally predicts what pleases everybody, whereas the prophet sent by God is as a rule bound to oppose what the people want (so esp. Jer. 28:8-9).

THE POWER OF GOD

Other stories put more emphasis on the power of the experience of God. When the spirit of God comes upon the prophet it sweeps him away against his will, perhaps taking him up to a mountain or over to a ravine where he might plunge to his death (1 Kings 18:12; 2 Kings 2:16; cf. Ezek. 3:12, 14; 8:3). In the case of Samson the spirit of God begins to stir him as young lad (Judg. 13:25). The spirit's power enables him to tear lions asunder and kill thirty of his enemies (14:6, 19). Samson can snap ropes apart and mow down a hundred men at a time with the jawbone of an ass (15:15-16). The prophet Elisha can divide the waters because Elijah's spirit has been given him (2 Kings 2:15). At first, amazement at such incredible, inexplicable deeds of power is very strong, and everything uncanny, inexplicable, and powerful, even when it is evil, is attributed to the spirit of God. Judges 9:23 and 1 Samuel 16:14; 18:10; 19:9 have no qualms in identifying an evil spirit sent upon the inhabitants of Shechem, and especially upon Saul, as coming from God. 1 Kings 22:20-23 describes a meeting of the heavenly council: a spirit comes forward and offers to go as a lying spirit and enter the false prophets because God is planning to bring calamity upon the people of Israel.

On the other hand we find that comparable experiences of the mighty help of God are not at all accompanied by such peculiar phenomena. We read, for instance, in the case of the judges that the spirit of God came upon them or took possession of them in order to help Israel assert its rights, to blow the trumpets and march against its foes (Judg. 3:10; 6:34; 11:29). Similar stories are told of Saul (1 Sam. 11:6) and of David (16:13). Even the political leadership of a nation is directed by the spirit of God, especially in times of famine or war, and can be described as an experience of his power. Yet, in the early days at least, justice, cultic laws, and general wisdom are not attributed to the spirit. As a general rule the spirit breaks in unexpectedly and moves people to do extraordinary things. It does not establish a permanent state of affairs.

WHAT DOES THIS MEAN?

In these experiences, some of them highly peculiar, one thing comes out clearly: the spirit of God is not simply the spirit of man, or an aspect of the human spirit. We can put it like this: "Man possesses a soul. The spirit possesses him."[1] In the spirit God is experienced at work in a worldly, earthly, and often even an outright political situation. But then, where else should man experience God's working? Yet it is not understood as a subjective experience but as the experience of an external power. It does not arise from man's own spirit but from a source which at first completely baffles him. Gradually, however, man becomes aware that this power might possibly be called "God!" Of course this awareness is no proof that the power experienced is not just an illusion. As in the case of human love, you cannot prove that it is not an illusion. But the distinction between God and his spirit on the one hand and man and his spirit on the other was of such great importance to Israel that the strangest tales were told about those who were seized by the spirit, even at a time when this type of phenomenon was being called into question and even repudiated.

Here, perhaps, is the most striking difference between Israel's experience and that of Eastern religions.[2] The God of the Old Testament is not the ultimate ground of being which we discover when we realize that we are one with the universe whose life and power is God himself. Nor is God simply the mystery at the heart of things, to be found in meditation, when we penetrate to the depths of the soul. In the Old Testament prophetic experience God encounters man as the completely Unexpected, whose strangeness and otherness in contrast to all that is human are the first characteristics man discovers. We need not be shocked when we hear of the strangeness of God in Eastern religions, nor conversely need we deny that for the devout of the Old Testament God is, as it were, the ground of all creation. But the Eastern and the biblical emphases are very different and that has many consequences in detail. Thus the Holy Spirit has nothing to do with the higher life of idealism which strives to elevate itself above the level of the material world. The Holy Spirit is as close to the body as to the soul, to the bodily functions of man as to his spiritual or psychic functions. Israel uses the same word for the spirit of God as it does for wind or storm. The spirit of God is as physical and concrete as the wind and storm which flatten trees and carry away roofs and whose effects can be felt in a highly physical way. What Israel experienced as the spirit of God transcends the distinction between material conditions and ideal, spiritual realms, between body and spirit or body and soul; it likewise transcends the divergent bourgeois and Marxist ideas of man and his world. One thing however seems typical of this spirit. It is never the spirit of conformism; that is, it never accomodates itself to its surroundings or shrinks from drawing attention to itself. On the contrary, it is the spirit which makes man stand on his own feet, even against all his contemporaries if necessary.

The Holy Spirit in Creation

THE SPIRIT OF GOD IN WIND AND STORM

Yet Israel could not stay where it was. In the hard times of the exile, reduced as it was to impotence, Israel learned to rely upon the power of the spirit and to realize ever more clearly that this power came from God himself. If God's presence and might were not limited to extraordinary, mysterious experiences or deeds of power, was it not then to be found in the whole of creation?

To begin with, this is certainly true for unique historical events. Thus we are told in the Song of Moses (Exod. 15:8, 10), (though in this form it was composed fairly late): "At the blast of thy nostrils the waters piled up" to enable Israel to go through the Red Sea; and again: "Thou didst blow with thy wind, and the sea covered them so that the enemy were destroyed." The word here translated "blast" is exactly the same word also rendered as "spirit." Israel thought of the spirit of God in such natural, concrete terms that it even recognized it in the east wind (14:21) which blew for a whole night just at the right time to make the shallowest part of the sea passable. Similarly we read in Genesis 8:1: "God made a wind blow over the earth, and the waters (of the flood) subsided."

But the spirit of God does not work only in such unique events of primordial history. Psalm 147:18 describes what takes place every spring when the thaw begins and the snows melt: "He makes his wind (or: spirit) blow, and the waters flow." In the warm breezes of spring the Israelite sees the presence and activity of God in his "spirit," which thaws the ice and snow. In the same way Isaiah 27:8 speaks of God's enemies: "He removed them with his fierce blast (or: spirit) in the day of the east wind."[3]

GOD'S SPIRIT AS
CREATIVE POWER

It is especially true for Genesis 1 that God's spirit is active in creation. The first chapter of the Bible was written quite late. Israel discovered the acts of God in the strange experiences of the prophets before it gave any explicit thought to his works in the routine and not so routine occurrences of nature.

We may ask which is the better translation of Genesis 1:2, "a mighty wind was moving over the face of the waters" [RSV margin], which would emphasize what is powerful and concrete in the expression, or "the Spirit of God was moving over the face of the waters" [RSV text], which would express what the narrator doubtless intends, namely, that God is at work here. Or might it be better simply to follow Martin Buber and speak of the "thunder of God" so as to do justice to both emphases? In any case neither can be understood without the other: what is here expressed as an operation of nature that can be observed and measured, is—and this cannot be simply observed or measured—nonetheless felt to be the activity of God.

15

It is self-evident to Israel as it is to Israel's neighbors that God created the world and man. That is why God's creation was never the object of a formal creed. But Israel's historical experience makes it conscious of God's action even where nothing extraordinary happens, as in the annual spring thaw, or where no human being is there to witness it, as in the creation of the world.

Anyone who understands this knows that Genesis 1 is not a description of the beginning of the world as we would find in a textbook of biology. The whole chapter is a testimony of faith. It sets forth in intelligible picture language what in the nature of the case is utterly unintelligible. It speaks of the work of God which we can never capture in our definitions, be they mathematical and scientific or more of a theological and dogmatic nature. It is the wind or spirit of God which stands behind the act of creation and operates in the separation of darkness and light, day and night, continents and seas. So things go wrong when man tries to blur the boundaries, when he calls light darkness and darkness light, good evil and evil good, when he turns night into day through frantic work and then sleeps all next day because he has nothing to do, when he cannot find any firm ground under his feet, or on the other hand, when he banishes from life the unknown and mysterious (which is what the sea was for the Israelites). What is said at the beginning of the Bible is expanded in the Psalms to cover the whole universe: "By the word of the Lord the heavens were made and all their host by the breath of his mouth" (33:6).

THE HOLY SPIRIT AS
LIFE-GIVING POWER

The most important development occurs when Israel begins consciously to describe all life including human life, as an expression of the spirit of God. Thus Psalm 104:29–30 says of the wild goats on the high mountains, of the young lions in the desert and of Leviathan, that strange monster of the sea: "When thou takest away their breath (or: spirit) they die . . . When thou sendest forth thy breath (or: Spirit) they are created" [RSV margin: breath; RSV text: Spirit]. Here the Spirit of God is pictured in very vivid terms. God exhales and his breath puts life into his creatures. God inhales and his breath is withdrawn from them and they die. Wherever life is awakened, it is the work of God's breath or Spirit. But where death occurs, it is *their* breath or spirit that departs. This is because God is concerned only with life. So the Bible does not like to refer to God's spirit in connection with death, although of course it is the same spirit or breath which entered God's creatures and so became "their spirit."

In Job 34:14–15 two different expressions are used: "If he should take back his spirit to himself, and gather to himself his breath, all flesh would perish together and man would return to dust." In connection with mankind the term "breath of life" is a particularly favorite expression, meaning man's life force, his God-given power to live. This is shown again in Job 27:3: "As long as my breath is in me, and the spirit of God is in my nostrils." Of course the two are the same, for God's spirit is in "my nostrils."

If the Israelite wishes to emphasize the source of life and to praise him who gives us this life, he speaks of the "spirit" of God. If on the other hand he wants to describe how man experiences this spirit of God in his life, he speaks of the "life-giving power," or the "breath of life." Genesis 2:7 tells how God breathed the "breath of life" into the nostrils of man, while 6:3 speaks of the "spirit" of God in man. Genesis 6:17 again refers to the "breath of life" and in 7:22 both expressions are combined: "breath of the spirit of life" [so literally the Hebrew, RSV omits "spirit"].

This "spirit of life" is also found in animals (Gen. 6:17; 7:15). All life, even the purely biological life force, is understood as the effect of the creative spirit of God: "Thus says the Lord, who stretched out the heavens and formed the spirit of man within him" (Zech. 12:1). This means that life never becomes a human possession, but always remains God's property — or better, God's action, God's creation. Thus God can say: "My spirit shall not abide in man forever . . . his days shall be a hundred and twenty years" (Gen. 6:3).

WHAT DOES THIS MEAN?

We are to understand that all life is a gift and not the work of our hands. It sometimes happens when we listen to a concert, that suddenly it ceases to be just a series of pleasant-sounding notes that we hear; instead it becomes real music, music that grips us, turns us inside out, and opens up new dimensions for us. Or we go on a hiking trip and suddenly sense the inexplicable wonder of everything about us, and we understand something of the secret that lies beyond the limited realm of what we can comprehend with our minds. That the Old Testament does not simply speak in a casual way of some unfathomable mystery, but specifically of the *Giver of this life* as "God" or as "the Lord" —well, we can understand that too, whether we agree with it or not.

Of course, this is a further step, and a decisive one which we may not find easy to take. Does this life really come from God? Is it not a mixture of all sorts of things, lofty and shallow, glorious and mean, good and bad? And when we think of ourselves, we know that what motivates us is often anything but divine, is in fact all too human. Or could it be that the purely biological is the divine part, spoiled only by the human will, by man's impulses, or by his mind? Yet will, impulse, and mind are as much a part of our biological make-up as sensitivity, instinct, and feeling.

The Old Testament had the same difficulty. This led to the formation of two distinct words which actually mean the same thing. Life can be viewed from two perspectives. On the one hand, it was created at the beginning and by God's will is meant to remain—in this connection the Old Testament speaks of "the spirit (of God)." On the other hand, life is that which men have made of it—in this connection the Old Testament speaks of the "life-giving power." Occasionally "my spirit" may mean the same thing as "my soul" (Isa. 26:9; Job 7:11), but in general "spirit" is seen as a power to which man succumbs at times of profound emotional experiences, as numerous Old Testament passages attest.[4]

This is shown by a further observation. The Old Testament Israelite does not divide a human being into two parts, one physical and the other psychological. He invariably considers the person a unified whole. Of course he can regard a human being from various angles. He can for example emphasize that man is at all times prone to sickness and death, in which case he

18

says: "Man is flesh." Or he may emphasize that man is receptive to life and all its opportunities, choosing one alternative or another and taking up this or that interest, in which case he says: "Man is soul." Therefore the expression "my flesh" or "my soul" often replaces the simple "I." But when this happens, the focus is either on the frailty which man shares with all creation, or on man's vital emotions.[5] But we never find the expression "my spirit" in place of "I." The Israelite cannot simply equate "the spirit" with himself. Does this then mean that the spirit is a higher element in human nature, or is it humanity viewed from a higher, more ideal perspective?

The Holy Spirit as the Source of Knowledge

SPIRIT AND FLESH

The Old Testament was aware that the life given by God can also be lived apart from God. And it may be the very "spirit" itself that is at fault. In the several passages referred to a moment ago (see note 4 above) mention is made of the impatient, jealous, and false spirits. This is very similar to what the prophets experienced. Where his emotions were concerned, what the Israelite first experienced was an incomprehensible power that came over him from time to time and that he attributed to the "spirit," without thereby clearly intending the Spirit of God as no more than one power among others. Even in the incomprehensible it is God who is at work: "The Lord your God hardened his spirit and made his heart obstinate" (Deut. 2:30). Of course there is an increasing emphasis on the fact of man's guilt: "those who err in spirit" (Isa. 29:24). A man who does not treasure the gift of God or ceases to regard it as God's gift has thus strayed away from him.

In no case then is the spirit of man to be regarded as the higher, purer, or more ideal part of him, and his body as the sinful part. "All flesh" is quickened by "the spirit" (Gen. 6:17; 7:15). Never is "flesh" evil or sinful in itself. "Flesh" is as much God's gracious gift as the spirit. The only thing that is evil or sinful is man, who puts his trust in the "flesh" alone instead of trusting in God, or who tries to base his life upon what he can touch and see, and no longer reckons with the fact that behind every visible and tangible reality there lies hidden the mystery of God. That, however, is the fault not of man's "flesh," but of his "heart," or actually his "spirit," because he "errs in spirit." Or again, it is the "spirit" which is obstinate because God has hardened it.[6] That is why the prophet can say: "Cursed is the man who trusts in man / and makes flesh his arm / whose heart turns away from the Lord" (Jer. 17:5). Hence 2 Chronicles 32:8 can say: "With him (the King of Assyria) is an arm of flesh, but with us it is the Lord our God." And that, too, is what Isaiah 31:3 means when it says: "The Egyptians are men, and not God; / and their horses flesh, and not spirit."

THE GIFT OF REASON

What we regard as of primary importance when we speak of the spirit, namely, the idea of a special power of reason, investigative activity, and perception, is not often mentioned in the Old Testament. This is how Job 32:8 understands the spirit:

> It is the spirit in a man,
>   the breath of the Almighty,
> that makes him understand.

Ten verses later this is described in the very picturesque lines:

> I am full of words,
>   the spirit within me constrains me.
> Behold, my heart is like wine that has no vent;
>   like new wineskins, it is ready to burst.

The Book of Job is one of those writings which deal with wisdom as it was ordinarily accessible to anyone who diligently looked for it. In the first passage quoted here the "spirit" is referred to as "the breath of the Almighty." Yet the second passage shows how closely related this is to the experience of the prophets, in which the spirit of God seizes a person unexpectedly, uninvited, and forces him to succumb. According to Deuteronomy 34:9 Joshua is filled by "the spirit of wisdom" because Moses had laid hands on him and so passed on to Joshua the spirit he had received from God himself. It is written of Daniel that he was filled by the holy spirit from God [RSV "the spirit of the holy gods"]. This does not simply mean reason in our sense of the word, but the God-given ability to interpret dreams and signs and to rule over a whole kingdom (Dan. 4:5; 5:11; 6:3), as was given earlier to Joseph by the spirit of God (Gen. 41:38). Again, in Malachi 2:15, where "spirit" could be translated "reason" it actually means the faith which remains true to the God of Israel. A late passage speaks of the "good Spirit" of God, meaning the One who teaches Israel (Neh. 9:20). But the same passage also speaks of the children of Israel being led (by the prophets, v. 30) in the desert. Similarly Isaiah 63:14 knows about the spirit of God which led Israel to rest although Israel constantly grieved God by rebelling against him. Here too it is above all Moses into whose heart God has put his holy spirit (vv. 10–11). An ill-advised political alliance which the prophet opposes is "not of my [God's] spirit" (Isa. 30:1). Thus it is taken for granted that God gives right judgment even in matters of politics (Isa. 30:1).

But nowhere does this simply mean ordinary human reason, for it is the "spirit" who conveys the knowledge of God or at any rate shows the way God intends both the individual and the whole people to follow. This must also be borne in mind in other passages where the "spirit" of man is roughly equivalent to what we mean by "expertise"; as for example, in Exodus 31:3 and 35:31, where God "filled" Bezalel "with ability and intelligence, with knowledge and all craftsmanship."

SPIRIT AND WORD

Hence it is a matter of crucial importance whether man lives his life intelligently. That need not be the same as living it "religiously." Any experience, perchance quite a "secular" one, may give us the courage to find ourselves, to discover our abilities, and at the same time to shun the spirit of conformity which supposes that the only right way to live is by agreeing with what everybody else says and does. "Secular" experiences may even make us "wise." They may give us the inner assurance, openness and flexibility to develop a meaningful life out of a frantic commitment to work or pleasure. It is also possible for an extraordinary yet still quite "secular" experience to surprise us in such a way that instead of just seeing a confusion of sights or hearing a confusion of sounds, we are suddenly able to sense something of the mystery of life as a whole. It would seem that

21

the Old Testament recognizes in all this something of what it calls life with God. Even that is the work of God's Spirit. He can be at work in Bezalel who makes artistic wood carvings and sets precious stones. He can be at work in Joseph and Daniel who govern a country wisely. He can be at work in the poet of the 104th psalm who is amazed at the wonders of nature and learns from it how to praise his Lord.

Yet it really makes a difference whether man recognizes it and gives thanks to the One who grants him such a life, or whether he never learns the lesson of gratitude. It is just this acknowledgement of God that his Spirit seeks to convey to us. That is why "Spirit" and "word" are so often used side by side:

> By the word of the Lord the heavens were made,
>> and all their host by the breath [or: spirit] of his mouth
>>> (Ps. 33:6)

> He sends forth his word and melts them,
>> he makes the wind [or: spirit] blow, and the waters flow
>>> (Ps. 147:18)

>> The Spirit of the Lord speaks by me,
>> his word is upon my tongue
>>> (2 Sam. 23:2)

> My spirit . . . is upon you, and my words . . . I have put in your mouth.
>> (Isa. 59:21)

While "Spirit" is a stronger expression for the overwhelming, often incomprehensible power of the divine event, "word" underscores the other side of it: God also enlightens and leads us to confess our faith in him, making us see clearly what he wills and does. That is why Jeremiah can say that the false prophets will become "wind" (or: spirit) and that the word is not in them (5:13). Job understood that, when he spoke of God's deeds and his Spirit [RSV wind] which was at work in them, and immediately continues: "Lo, these are the outskirts of his ways; / and how small a whisper do we hear of him" (26:14). Obviously the author of the Book of Job has already recognized the modern problem: God's action in creation may be powerful, it may cause amazement, yet the "word" within it which points to the Creator and helps us to learn to pronounce his name is so quiet that many are unable to hear it. The Spirit reaches its goal only when it becomes identical with the "word." Therefore man can take courage and not rest content with a vague feeling, but recognize that there is a mystery here, and learn to give it utterance:

> I praise thee, for thou art fearful and wonderful.
> Wonderful are thy works!
>
> (Ps. 139:14)

WHAT DOES THIS MEAN?

The problem Israel had to wrestle with is this: God's Spirit was to be found, on the one hand, everywhere in creation, and on the other hand, in the experiences of the prophets as an "alien" power that descends upon man. The answer, already adumbrated by the Old Testament, is that all of life, its sensuousness and its joy, is the good creation of God's Spirit. But this does not mean that man recognizes creation as the gift of God. For if man is absorbed in all the richness of created life and forgets who gave it, he is then putting the "flesh" in the place which belongs to the Creator of all flesh, to God and his Spirit. Then man has forfeited his life. He wanders into those boundless wastes where he can heap riches upon riches, honor upon honor, frantic effort upon frantic effort, sexual experience upon sexual experience, forgetting that it must all be accepted as God's good gift. Then God will suddenly withdraw the breath of life and all is over. But such insight no man can discover from his own resources. It too is the gift of God's Spirit. This is shown in a spectacular way in the experience of the prophets. God's Spirit forces them into an entirely new direction which they would never have thought of by themselves. In the last resort the same thing happens whenever man freely accepts the gift of true wisdom, for example, for his work, as did Bezalel. But the same is true of his leisure time and all the enjoyment it brings.

So the crucial point — and Israel learned this only gradually — is not whether such insight comes upon us in some extraordinary way. It does not even matter whether it is properly speaking a religious experience or not. What matters is whether man makes "flesh" his foundation, whether he bases his life on things he can control, like his bank account or the power he wields in the economy, the atom bomb, or his learning, oratory, artistic gifts, or whatever. What matters is that he base his life upon the "spirit," that he understand his life as a gift he can never wrest by force. Only so can he discover its secret. And that will make him open to the One who stands behind this gift and its secret, the One whose name the Spirit seeks to teach us. Perhaps this truth is nowhere so profoundly expressed as in Psalm 139:7: "Whither shall I go then from thy Spirit? / Or whither shall I flee from thy presence?" Whoever prays those words has learned to discern in his own life the "face" of God looking upon him with favor. He has learned that this is where he encounters God's "Spirit" which puts into his heart the response: "I thank thee because I am marvellously made" (v. 14) [BCP version], and at the same time the prayer:

> Search me, O God, and know my heart!
> . . . .
> And see if there be any wicked way in me,
> and lead me in the way everlasting!
>
> (vv. 23–24)

The Holy Spirit in the Future Consummation

THE SPIRIT AS THE CREATOR OF A NEW WORLD

It is primarily the major prophets who recognize that God and his Spirit are not bound to the world as man sees it. Something of this breadth of outlook comes out in that curious chapter at the beginning of Ezekiel. There we read of a vision the prophet had which he could hardly express in words. On a certain day in July 593 B.C. God appeared to him and called him to be his prophet. The first thing Ezekiel saw in this vision was a stirring of the spirit, descending like a storm from the north (Ezek. 1:4). The spirit drove a cloud before it and in that cloud came four living creatures in the form of men, each with four faces and four wings. After them came four wheels moving in all directions, even straight up, without turning. Twice the prophet tells us that these creatures went wherever the spirit took them (1:12, 20). Then above them God appeared to him in person, in radiant glory. Now it is not necessary to make sense of every detail in this vision, let alone offer a psychological interpretation of it. The important point is that the Old Testament is aware of a world, beyond the reach of man, where the Holy Spirit reigns. What this whole series of pictures tells us, surpassing as they do all description and defying all imagination, is the way the prophet is overwhelmed when he sees this divine world, far transcending what man with his senses can either see or understand. We might call it a world beyond the universe open to our exploration, but we must not take this in a spatial or geographical sense. Indeed this world of God is experienced by Ezekiel within his own earthly world. This means a life where God holds sway, a life beyond what we can normally see or recognize. At the same time the prophet sees that this world of infinity, hidden and mysterious though it is to us, is not sheer chaos, however chaotic the images may appear which force themselves upon our consciousness. It is replete with God's order; God's Spirit determines what is to happen there.

But this means that God's Spirit is able to work in ways quite different from what we can imagine. That is something we must not forget if we want to look into the future. When the prophets look into the future what they foresee is primarily God's judgment, when God will vindicate the right which man has denied him. Once more, it is the Spirit of God that is at work here. Yet the future is still thought of in historical terms. Thus Isaiah expects that the Spirit of God will fall upon Israel's enemies like an overflowing stream reaching up to the neck. Then the Spirit will gather the wild beasts in the desert (Isa. 30:28; 34:16).[7] The same judgment might come upon Israel if it refuses to turn back to God. The east wind will come, the "wind (spirit) of the Lord" from the desert, and dry up all the land (Hos. 13:15). But conversely, the same wind or spirit may turn the desert into a paradise. This obviously means a time of salvation when everything will be changed, even the geography and the climate:

> until the Spirit is poured upon us from on high,
> and the wilderness becomes a fruitful field. . . .
> . . . .
> And the effect of righteousness will be peace,
> and the result of righteousness,
> quietness and truth for ever.
>
> (Isa. 32:15–17)

> I will pour water on the thirsty land,
>   and streams on the dry ground;
> I will pour my Spirit upon your descendants,
>   and my blessing on your offspring.
>
> (Isa. 44:3)

Which is it to be now, judgment or blessing? Joel 2:28–32 describes the coming day of judgment which clearly brings this world and its order to an end. It is "the great and terrible day of the Lord" on which "the sun shall be turned to darkness, and the moon to blood." Then God will pour his Spirit upon all, and whoever calls upon his name will be saved, for upon Mount Zion and in Jerusalem there will be salvation. Still more plainly Isaiah 4:4 tells us: A spirit of judgment will come upon Jerusalem. Like an overflowing stream it will wash away all the filth and all the guilt, leaving behind a cleansed and holy people to live in peace and prosperity.

THE SPIRIT AS THE CREATOR OF A NEW HUMANITY

By now it is clear that the new world which the Spirit will create is dependent on the transformation of man.

Quite early on, the author of Psalm 51 wrote:

> Create in me a clean heart, O God,
>   and put a new and right spirit within me.
> . . . .
> and take not thy holy Spirit from me.
>
> (vv. 10–11)

But this is perhaps the only place in the Old Testament which states that God will give his Spirit, not just for some specific need but as an abiding presence, to everyone who asks for it. Numbers 11:29 says that Moses cried out: "Would that all the Lord's people were prophets, that the Lord would put his spirit upon them (and not only on the seventy elders)." But this is only a pious hope, and unfortunately it is not the way things happen in the present. This is what Joel looks for in the glorious future. Everybody, sons and daughters, old men and young men, men servants and maid servants, will prophesy as God himself gives them utterance. Similarly, Zechariah foretells that when the end comes God will "pour out . . . a spirit of grace [KJV] and supplication" (Zech. 12:10). The clearest expression of these future expectations is found in Ezekiel. The prophet sees a valley full of dry bones. With a rattling noise the Spirit of God comes upon them and makes them come alive again. They are not covered again with sinews and flesh and skin; they are filled with the Spirit of God. They come alive and all recognize God as Lord (Ezek. 37:1–14). This is not just the breath of life which God breathed into man at the beginning (Gen. 2:7).[8] Now of course all this is just picture language for the restoration of Israel on the historical plane. Yet at the same time it is already a vision of possibilities hitherto undreamed of which God offers. God's Spirit can even open "graves" and bring out the dead (Ezek. 37:12). When God's Spirit is poured over the people and they all recognize him as their Lord (39:28–29) a new world will come into being. The real renewal of the world comes not with a change of outward conditions, as in irrigation of the deserts; it comes when God washes away all evil and gives mankind a new heart and a new spirit; his own spirit, and enables men to live according to his laws (11:19–20; 36:25–27).

WHAT DOES THIS MEAN?

For the great prophets of Israel the Holy Spirit first came alive in their experiences of the past (for example, in their calling). But how strange! Scarcely have they realized that God has chosen them through his Spirit to a special destiny, when they are no longer satisfied with that. God's Spirit has also been at work in the history of the people as a whole, drying up the Red Sea for Israel to pass through, destroying Israel's enemies, and leading the people for forty years through the desert. But again, how strange! No sooner have the prophets begun to understand that God's Spirit had prepared the way for his people, than they are once again no longer satisfied.

> Pass over to Calneh, and see;
>   and thence go to Hamath the great;
>   then go to Gath of the Philistines.
> Are they better than these kingdoms?
> . . . .

> Did I not bring Israel from the land of Egypt,
> and the Philistines from Caphor and the Syrians from Kir?
> (Amos 6:2; 9:7)

In other words, God is not only at work in Israel and its history, he is at work in other nations as well. He has a purpose for the whole world.

This has implications for the future. One cannot live exclusively in the past, even if that past involves a constitutive experience of God. One cannot look back all the time to one's conversion or special calling. God's Spirit wants to go forward. He wants to accompany us into the future, and Israel must learn to live out of this future. Israel's ideas of God's Spirit must change, until it understands that the Spirit seeks to build a new world in which justice and peace shall reign. The strange thing here is that the prophets first had to transmit the message that this Spirit of a new world would come upon man as a storm of judgment, sweeping away all before it. True, this will happen to others as well, but especially to those people to whom the prophet was sent. Only where man is receptive to this judgment and accepts the gift of a new heart and a new spirit, can God's Spirit build a new world. Of course, God wants more than a few converted souls — he wants to create a whole new world. But this can happen only if individuals first surrender themselves to this Spirit and yield to his judgment. It is like the setting of a watch: it has to be constantly checked and adjusted to the right time. Only those who submit to the rule of God's Spirit will bring justice and peace.

This is how the Old Testament reveals the future God intends. The New Testament then will take up the story. But before we come to that we must briefly discuss the intertestamental period.

3

The Spirit in Intertestamental Judaism

From 538 B.C. on Israel lived under persian rule, and from 332 B.C. on, under "Hellenistic" rule, first Greek, then Egyptian, and then Syrian, though from 63 B.C. on it had come increasingly under Roman rule. Change in rulership brought with it entirely new views of the world, especially in the field of religion.

The newer Greek thought patterns were, as usual, not always in accord with the older traditional expressions of faith, and the question naturally arose: Where is restatement essential, and where should the old be preserved? What is merely a matter of outward expression, open to change where necessary, and what belongs to the heart of the matter? The questions posed then were much like the questions posed now when patterns of thought change.

Unlike Hebrew or Aramaic as it was spoken at the time of Jesus, the Greek language draws a clear distinction between wind, human reason, and spirit. "Spirit" is defined in strictly scientific terms as a current of air or breath, at once the object and source of motion. Two Greek theories became especially influential in Judaism. One was Stoicism, which conceives the universe as a monistic, well-ordered whole. Everything within this universe is permeated by the spirit of God, which fills everything like a kind of electric current. The spirit is present in weaker measure in plants and stones, more potently in animals, and most of all in humanity, especially in human reason. But the same spirit is also at work in the structures of the universe. It rules the stars in their courses and keeps the world from disintegrating. This Stoic view was completely different from the earlier view of Plato who held that the human soul is imprisoned in an earthly body as in a tomb, from which it escapes only by death to rise again to its heavenly home, though Plato of course did not speak of "spirit" but of "soul."

In the first century B.C. these two philosophies, Platonic and Stoic, take a new lease on life and give rise to a remarkable new theory. For centuries at Delphi there had been a priestess who uttered oracles. Her special knowledge is now scientifically explained: She was sitting on top of a crack in the earth's surface from which certain vapors issued forth and penetrated into her brain; these vapors, charged with a divine "spirit" related to the soul of man, inspired the priestess with a special "divine knowledge." It was a case of God playing on the soul of the priestess as on a zither or a flute. Here too the spirit is regarded as a natural force, a sort of material substance of which the soul is constituted, or which worked in and through the soul.

The Holy Spirit as the Stranger:
The Problem of the Prophetic Experience

SCRIPTURE

Not even in this intertestamental period did the people of Israel forget that God had spoken to them chiefly through the prophets. God was not the summit of human thought in its ceaseless quest for greater understanding. He was a God who irrupted unexpectedly as a stranger, at first unwelcome, into the world of men. But how peculiar were many of those strange occurrences! Where was the dividing line between the true prophet and those noisy charlatans who, whether consciously or unconsciously, proclaimed their own dreams and ideas in the name of God? The official theology answered these questions by recognizing only those prophets whose writings were in the Bible: "When Haggai, Zechariah, and Malachi, the last of the prophets, died, the Holy Spirit departed from Israel," declares one rabbi[1] and already Psalm 74:9 (written perhaps between 168 and 165 B.C.) assets: "There is no longer any prophet, / and there is none among us who knows how long." In a Jewish document of the end of the first century A.D. we read: "The prophets have fallen asleep" (Syr. Bar. 85:3).

Unfortunately life does not always abide by the wise and

prudent sayings of the theologians. As a matter of fact, there appeared at this time a series of prophets very similar to those in ancient Israel. The "Teacher of Righteousness" who founded the Jewish monastic order of Qumran by the Dead Sea certainly ranks with the prophets of the Old Testament, but all he does is to discover the meaning of the prophecies which had been hidden from the original prophets at the time (1 QpHab 7:1–5). In other words, it was to the founder of this sect that the meaning of the prophecies was revealed. Josephus tells us that in this group there was a regular school of prophets (*Ant.* 13. 311 ff.). He also speaks of a group of prophets at the court of Herod (*Ant.* 17. 43 ff.) and of many individuals who performed all kinds of miracles, often attracting to themselves thousands of followers. One of these is said to have cried out for seven years and five months, "Woe unto Jerusalem" (*Ant.* 20. 97–98; 169 ff.; *War* 6. 300 ff.; 7. 347 ff.). Three prophets are mentioned in the canonical Book of Acts (5:36–37; 21:28). It is apparently not so simple to channel the Holy Spirit and confine him to officially approved reservations. On the contrary, what happened here is the same as what happened in the history of the church: the more the official leaders tried to regiment and incorporate the Holy Spirit into their systems, the stronger was the rise from below of those strange figures who, though they were not accepted and for that very reason could not be controlled or be reminded of their limits, yet fascinated people all the more.

INSPIRATION

Philo, a contemporary of Jesus living in Alexandria, tackled the problem in an entirely different way. As a philosopher he was far more influenced by Greek scientific thinking than those who lived in Palestine. He developed an original theory of prophetic experience and maintained that there is no such thing as real wisdom without such experience. When the Old Testament asserts that God meets the prophets as a stranger, Philo reads this in terms of Platonic philosophy. There is a higher, divine world, and a lower, material one in which the divine can only live as in a prison. The only way to real knowledge is for all human knowledge and understanding to be extinguished. As soon as the divine light appears that of man fades away (*Who is the Heir* 265). Where reason disappears, mystic trance and ecstasy take its place. Another—God himself—takes charge of the prophet's mouth or tongue (*On Dreams* 2. 252). When that happens, the soul prophesies things of which it knows not (*On the Cherubim* 27; cf. *On the Migration of Abraham* 34–35; *On the Change of Names* 39). Philo describes just such an experience: "I . . . seemed always to be borne aloft into the heights with a soul possessed by some God-sent inspiration, a fellow-traveller with the sun and moon and the whole heaven and the universe. Ah, then I gazed down from the upper air . . . and beheld . . . the multitudinous world-wide spectacles of earthly things, and blessed my lot in that I had escaped . . . from the plagues of mortal life . . . I got me wings . . . and am irradiated by the light of wisdom" (*On the Special Laws* 3. 1).

From the true insight that man should be conscious of his limitations, especially because he can run away from God and live against God's will, there develops, quite unintentionally, the utterly un-Jewish notion that the material world is evil, quenching everything that is divine. The Holy Spirit and man's spirit are no longer differentiated in the sense that the human spirit is free to refuse to obey God and his Spirit. They are now polarized, in absolute opposition to each other: when one arrives the other must vanish. Conversely, there is a higher world where everything that happens is divine. No question is raised as to whether or not such experiences at their profoundest level are just human possibilities, having no more connection with God than other experiences. That is why Philo can also speak of the divine spirit in man. Since it is purely human reason it must of course give way when God speaks. Yet at the same time there is in man a higher, divine part which then becomes manifest (cf. pp. 39–40).

Of course the Old Testament prophet also realized that he was given the decisive knowledge; he does not simply discover it on his own, but God speaks to him in the midst of this earthly world. God shows Amos a basket of ripe fruit and shows him how autumn has fallen upon Israel too, and that God is going to send a hard winter (Amos 8:1–2). He shows Jeremiah the injustice which is going on in Jerusalem, and lets him see in that injustice the imminence of God's judgment (Jer. 5:1–9). He makes Isaiah analyze the political situation and warns him against the party which sets its hopes on foreign alliances (Isa. 31:1–9). There is no sign that human thinking has come to an end. On the contrary, Isaiah and Jeremiah, for example, used their God-given insight to ponder what all this might mean for the political and social situation of their country. Amos and Micah acutely observed every instance of economic and social injustice. Hosea and Malachi protested against concrete instances of corruption among the priesthood.

EVIL

An even sharper dilemma was posed by Old Testament passages that attribute evil to the Spirit, sometimes in quite explicit terms. Even Satan, according to Job, is a servant of God (1:6–12)—he can act only according to God's will. It is the same with the evil spirit in 1 Kings 22:19–23, and Amos says: "Does evil befall a city, unless the Lord has done it?" (3:6). Later on these statements become increasingly reserved and finally disappear. Israel has learned to take human sin seriously even in those cases where evil comes over a man like a strange, uncanny power.

For the official teachers of Israel during the post–Old Testament period the freedom of the human will is all-important. Man has two impulses, one good and the other evil, but he has the freedom to choose between the two. The Holy Spirit or soul was given to him by God at the moment of birth and it is man's task to give back this Holy Spirit or soul clean and pure at the end of his life.

Even the Greek translators of the Old Testament are cautious here. While 1 Samuel 16:23 speaks quite freely of "the evil spirit from God" that came upon Saul and drove him mad, the Greek translators speak merely of "an evil spirit," without attributing it to God.

Yet there are other solutions available, of quite a different kind. The Old Testament itself speaks of pagan deities, once even of the "great wrath" of a pagan god that "came upon Israel" (2 Kings 3:27). Above all, Israel is aware of desert spirits who have to be bought off with a sin offering (Lev. 16:8–10), and of the spirits of the dead who obey certain soothsayers (1 Sam. 28:7). This becomes increasingly important in the intertestamental period, not least of all as a result of Israel's centuries-long contact with the Persian religion and its doctrine that the world had been ruled from primordial times by a good spirit and an evil spirit, both of which have their agents fighting for the control of mankind. Ideas like these emerge most clearly in the Qumran community where we hear of the two spirits, or angels, who wrestle for the control of man (1QS 3:18 ff.; 4:23 ff.; CD 5:18). The same ideas are to be found in the Jewish work called the *Testaments of the Twelve Patriarchs* but with the addition of an intermediate spirit, "a spirit of the understanding of the mind," that shows men which direction they should turn (Judah 20:1–2). In a Christian writing of the second century A.D. the good spirit is equated with the Holy Spirit or with the virtues, and the evil spirit with the bad conscience of man or with his vices (Shepherd of Hermas, *Man.* 3:4; 5:2, 5, 7; 10:1, 2; *Sim.* 9:13, 2, 7). But the crucial point is that even now Judaism firmly clings to the belief that both spirits, the good as well as the evil, were created by God (1QS 3:25). Mention of evil spirits becomes more frequent (for example, Tob. 6:8; Wisd. 7:20) while Josephus sees in the demons the souls of departed sinners (*War* 7. 7,185).[2]

EVALUATION

In the Old Testament the strangeness of the Spirit was most apparent in the experiences of the prophets. Two attempts are now made to solve the problem in contemporary Judaism, but neither does justice to the reality of the Holy Spirit. The Spirit cannot be restricted to what the Old Testament prophets had said of him, all of which had since been written down and officially accepted as biblical truth. For the Holy Spirit is still alive at the present time and cannot be simply preserved as an event of the past. Just how impossible this is is also shown by the realization, still very much alive in the intertestamental period, that the Holy Spirit is still needed, even if only to comprehend fully what the prophets were saying in an older day and apply it to the entirely different problems of the present. Conversely, however, one could not describe past manifestations of the

Spirit in exclusively psychological terms and then attribute similar psychological phenomena in contemporary life to the Holy Spirit. We know today just how impossible such an explanation would be because drugs can cause quite similar experiences. This leaves open the question as to just how the Holy Spirit is to be recognized and distinguished from all other experiences, and how both aspects can be combined: the crucial significance of the Old Testament prophets and the freedom of the Spirit to speak anew today.

The legacy of the Old Testament includes yet another problem. The Old Testament is aware that in creation there is both good and evil, but it leaves the origin of evil unexplained—even in the story of the Fall. But man learns of evil in two ways. On the one hand he knows of his guilt: this is what he chose, though he could have chosen differently; therefore he must take seriously the freedom he has been given and speak of his own evildoing. On the other hand he experiences evil irresistibly overcoming him, sometimes even without his recognizing it for what it is; therefore he must acknowledge the overwhelming power of evil. Evil can enslave a person, even an entire nation; in fact it can enslave a whole era. Hence man is obliged to speak of "the spirit" of evil. Both of these understandings of evil were underscored by Judaism in New Testament times. On the one hand it emphasized man's gift of free will and attributed everything to his own decisions. On the other hand it constantly talked about an evil spirit or spirits engaged in battle against God, exercising their power alongside God as well as against him, with man bounced like a ball between two players. But the question of how the two views are to be reconciled with each other remains unanswered. Is there alongside the Holy Spirit such a thing as an evil spirit? Or is it really only human disobedience against the Holy Spirit of God?

The Holy Spirit in Creation:
God's Presence in the World

The idea that God's Spirit is active in creation recedes at this time, though there is still an echo of Psalm 33:6: "O Thou . . . who hast fixed the firmament by the word, and hast made the light of the heaven by thy spirit" (Syr. Bar. 21:4). It is also known that the Spirit of God's power, even a single breath of this Spirit, can destroy dreadful monsters, "such as breathe out fiery breath" (Wisd. 11:18–20). But real pronouncements about the creative power of God become rare. Rather, the "wisdom" of God appears as the source of all things (Wisd. 7:21–22). According to Sirach 24:3, wisdom proceeds from the mouth of God and covers the earth like a mist (cf. Gen. 1:2).[3] Sometimes it is the Spirit which continues to work in nature. God is not like a clockmaker who started everything ticking at the beginning and then went into retirement. Hence Judaism of that time pictured the angels of God, his "ministering spirits" (Heb. 1:14), as the moving force behind all nature. According to Psalm 104:4 God makes the winds his angels and flames of fire his ministers. The Greek translator appears to understand it the other way around, that God transforms his angels into winds (or "spirits") and his servants into flames of fire. That is certainly the way the Jewish sages of the time always interpret it.[4] These angels or spirits hold the storehouses of the winds, the power of the moonlight, all categories of stars, the sea, hoarfrost, snow, fog, dew, rain, thunder, and lightning in their power. They are able to open the reservoir which holds the raindrops, and to whip up or keep tight rein on the thunder and lightning, so that they always go into action at the same time (*Eth. Enoch* 60:11–23; similarly *Jub.* 2:2; further Strack-Billerbeck 3, 818–820).

On the other hand modern enlightened Jews could no longer talk about angels turning on faucets and making the rain fall. Yet they wanted to hold onto the idea of the work of the Spirit of God. So they adopted the Stoic notion of the divine Spirit considered as a force of nature, pervading all things and holding them together: "The Spirit of the Lord fills [RSV has filled] the world" (Wisd. 1:7). Philo in particular speaks of the Spirit as the bond which holds together the wood and stones and makes them solid. This is the "all-uniting" spirit which is to Philo the highest and already divine "element" (*Who is the Heir* 242; *On the Creation* 131). Philo can describe the superiority of God and his activity in quite a scientific way. The Spirit of God forms the topmost layer, the one which lies above earth, water, and atmosphere, and forms the "heavens," the world of God. Yet at the same time it gives cohesion to everything on earth, and thus transforms it into a "universe" (*On Drunkenness* 106; *On the Special Laws* 4. 123).

But here, too, much is left open. The only thing that becomes clear is that both points have to be made. On the one hand God's Holy Spirit is present in all natural phenomena, the glorious as well as the dreadful ones. On the other hand the freedom of God stands above the whole development of nature and guides it; this is a truth that must not disappear in favor of some impersonal natural power which is then deified. How can both ideas be expressed without doing injustice to one of them?

The Holy Spirit as the Source of Knowledge: The Human Spirit

THE EXPOSITION OF THE
BIBLICAL STATEMENTS
ABOUT THE SPIRIT

This is where the most difficult questions emerge. The teachers of Palestinian Jewry noticed the dangers that arise if the human soul or reason is simply equated with God's Holy Spirit. Therefore, wherever the Old Testament speaks of "Spirit" they prefer the more innocuous word, "breath of life."[5] In Josephus the term "spirit," in the sense of the human spirit, almost completely disappears. At the very most he states that "soul and spirit" (probably conceived as material substances) are located "in the blood" (*Ant.* 3.260).[6] Conversely, the Greek translators often render "breath of life" or "life" as "spirit" (1 Kings 17:17; Job 34:14; Dan. 5:23; 10:17; Isa. 38:12). This is no accident. For if they accepted the Stoic view that the world is permeated by a divine Spirit as a kind of natural force, the only way they could explain the Old Testament teaching about the Spirit of God in man was to say that the all-pervading Spirit finds its strongest concentration in the human soul or reason. Thus we read in Wisdom 7:22-26: "Wisdom (the source of all things) . . . is a spirit[7] that is intelligent, holy, . . . overseeing all, / and penetrating through all spirits. . . . / because of her pureness she pervades and penetrates all things. / For she is a breath of the power of God, / and a pure emanation of the glory of the

Almighty; / . . . a reflection of eternal light." Of course the real problem is immediately obvious. In the very next verse we read: "She passes (only) into holy souls / and makes them friends of God, and prophets (v. 27). Again, according to 7:7, "the spirit of wisdom," that is, "reason," is given to the person who asks God for it, while according to 9:17 the only person who perceives the will of God is the one to whom the Lord gives "Wisdom," that is, "his Holy Spirit from on high." Hard by this however we find the other notion, that God has "inspired him with an active soul and has breathed into him a living spirit" (15:11).

SPIRIT AND FLESH

The difficulties become still more evident where people think in terms of the Platonic contrast between a heavenly soul and an earthly, material body. Where people still adhere closely to the biblical message they will avoid the contrast between flesh and spirit, body and soul. The teachers of Israel generally emphasize that it is precisely the combination of the spirit with the body that constitutes the act of God's creation, even if they hold with Genesis 2:7 that the body is from the earth, while the spirit is breathed in by God and so derives from heaven. The ascensions to heaven of men of outstanding piety occur "in the body" or "in the spirit." Both refer to the same kind of experience, only the emphasis varies, being placed either on the concrete occurrence or on the power which effects it.[8] When Judith 10:13 says "neither flesh nor spirit of life," the two expressions are synonymous. Similarly, in Sirach 14:16–17 it says, "Beguile your soul . . . yet all flesh will die" [author's translation] and it means in each case "deceive yourself . . . (like all men) you also will pass away." The Hebrew text of Isaiah 31:3 says that the Egyptians are "men and not God," and that their horses are "flesh and not spirit." This means that they are limited in their strength. In the meantime however people had heard of Platonic philosophy, in which the material body was regarded as a burden and as evil, and only the invisible soul was divine. A literal translation would therefore now be misunderstood. That is why the Greek translators speak of the "flesh" of the horses in which there is no help, without mentioning the contrast between

38

flesh and "spirit." By avoiding a literal translation they have reproduced exactly what the prophetic text originally intended.

But this did not happen everywhere. Numbers 16:22 and 27:16 say in the Hebrew text, "God of the spirits of all flesh," for everything that is flesh has also received the spirit of life. But the Greek Bible draws a distinction between the realm of the spirit and that of the flesh. God is now "Lord of the spirits *and* of all flesh." As early as the second century B.C. we read in the Jewish Book of *Jubilees* that God created the spirits on the first day whereas bodily beings were created only on the fifth day (2:2–11). Also the strange story in Genesis 6:1–4 is now understood to imply that the angels, who as "living spirits" descended from heaven to earth and joined in union with the "blood of flesh" of earthly women, caused children to be born who were no longer according to the spirit but according to the flesh (*Eth. Enoch* 15:4; 106:17). Similarly Wisdom 7:1–2 understands man as "flesh," created from "seed" and "pleasure," while the "spirit of wisdom" has to be added later (v. 7). Again 4 Maccabees 7:13–14 distinguishes flesh, sinews, and muscles from the spirit of reason. The clearest instance, however, is the distinction made by Philo between those human beings who live only "by blood and the pleasure of the flesh" and those who live "by reason, the divine inbreathing" (*Who is the Heir* 55–58). In contrast to the "clod of earth" and the "pleasure of the flesh" (ibid.), the "divine spirit" points upwards and bears the "reason" thither (*On Noah's Work as a Planter* 23–24). The fleshly nature therefore has no part in the spirit (*The Worse Attacks the Better* 84). Only the disembodied, noncorporeal soul can perceive the disembodied, noncorporeal God (*On the Unchangeableness of God* 52–56; *On the Giants* 31). Hence the servants of the spirit are pale, almost disembodied wraiths like mere skeletons who ignore all the attachments of the flesh (*On the Special Laws* 4. 114; *On the Giants* 30; *On the Change of Names* 32–33). The flesh and its lusts are opposed to piety and the knowledge of God (*On Dreams* 2. 67; *On the Change of Names* 143), for flesh is sin and servitude, the coffin and funeral urn of the soul (*Who is the Heir* 268; *On the Unchangeableness of God* 31). Similarly we read in a passage as early as Wisdom 9:15: "The [RSV A] perishable body weighs down the soul, / and this earthly tent burdens the thoughtful mind." The teaching of Plato about the divine soul being imprisoned in the material body has clearly upset the balance of the biblical views. Of course the Bible generally speaks of "spirit" and "flesh" rather than of "soul" and "body." But the "spirit" or divine "breath" is equated with "reason," the highest part of the soul in Plato, whereas the mere life force resides in the blood and is to be found even in animals (*The Worse Attacks the Better* 83). In other places this "divine spirit" is simply equated with the "soul" which God breathed into man according to Genesis 2:7 (*On the Creation* 135, 144). These conflicting and contradictory statements of Philo prove how difficult he finds it to harmonize the biblical view with his modern Greek ideas about man.

EVALUATION

The difficulties already suggested in the Old Testament now come clearly to the fore. Can it be said that the biological life of man (and perhaps that of animals too) is identical with the Holy Spirit? Or can this be said only of the "soul," whatever that might mean? Or could this identification of man's life with the Holy Spirit perhaps be accepted at least with respect to man's power of reason as opposed to mere animal instinct? Or is it true only of very special expressions of this power, for example, of genuine human wisdom, or perhaps man's religious perception of God? And in that case what is the connection between this human capacity of endowment and what the Holy Spirit says to a person on special occasions, for example, in the call of a prophet? We can gauge how unclear these assertions are by the fact that the soul is regarded as a gift of God, though as a sort of permanent loan which can be cancelled. Alternatively, reason was breathed into man by God but true wisdom is found only where the fear of God prevails, and that can only be a gift from him. In addition, according to Philo it is divine inspiration, not reason, that gives real knowledge of God. Should one therefore 1) with Plato distinguish a celestial, divine part of man, his "soul" or "spirit," from the material (and therefore evil) body, the "flesh" which imprisons him? Or should one 2) rather, influenced by the Old Testament, assume that all God's creatures in heaven, that is, the angels and perhaps the souls of the departed, are pure and holy, whereas all flesh is sinful? Or should one 3) follow Persian thought and distinguish between good and evil spirits that respectively influence good and evil men on earth? All three alternatives forget the biblical truth that God created the soul or spirit of man, and that he alone is God and Creator. True, the Bible believes that all flesh has its limitations and is exposed to the threat of death. But that applies equally to the human spirit. Of course the flesh is exposed to every kind of temptation, but is it not the human spirit which is the source of these temptations, and itself subject to them? Or should one 4) distinguish on the one hand between a "spirit" in man that comes from God and is destined to return to its home or to a higher life—whether we think in this connection of man's biological life or of the capacities of the human soul—and on the other hand what man makes of that spirit? The question remains unanswered, and the following chapter points up still greater difficulties.

The Holy Spirit in the Future Consummation: The Problem of the Resurrection

THE MESSIAH

Just as Judaism at that time speaks little of the activities of the Spirit throughout creation and concentrates rather on the individual, so too in the expression of its ideas about the future. There is an expectation of the Messiah who will reign "mightily in Spirit" (Ps Sol. 17:37; 18:7), who will be endowed with God's glory and with the spirit of understanding, holiness, and grace (T. Levi 18:7; T. Judah 24:2). In one passage (which may however be post-Christian) we even hear of the "Son of man" upon whom the "Spirit of righteousness" is poured out, enabling him to destroy all sinners (Eth. Enoch 62:2).

IMMORTALITY OF THE SOUL?

The belief now becomes prevalent that the soul or spirit of man will survive death. When Psalm 16:10 expresses the conviction that God will not give up the soul of the Psalmist to the underworld, that is, will not let him die but have him recover, the Greek translators most likely understand this to mean "Thou wilt not leave my soul in Hades," thus presupposing that after the death of the body the soul enters another world where God keeps it in safety. Psalm 22:30 speaks (in the Hebrew) of the "soul which lives no longer," whereas the Greek translators speak of "the soul which lives in him (God)." But it should be remembered that the Hebrew word for "not" sounds almost the same as the word for "him." The Preacher in the Old Testament asks, perhaps skeptically, "Who knows whether the spirit of man goes upward and the spirit of the beast down to the earth?" (Eccles. 3:21), and claims that no one knows "how the spirit comes to the bones in the womb of a woman with child" (11:5). The author therefore must have reflected on the belief that all life is really a God-given spirit, and come increasingly to doubt it. Who knows just how this spirit enters the embryo within the womb of a pregnant mother? And who can tell what happens to it after death? If the spirit of a man rises up to God, why not also the spirit of animals?

Similarly, the mother of the seven pious Jewish sons who were martyred for their faith says she does not know how they were created within her womb. She knows only that she had not given them "the spirit and the life." And on the strength of this she argues confidently that the Creator of the world will give them "spirit and life" again after their death (2 Macc. 7:22–23). Still more confident is Wisdom 12:1: "Thy immortal spirit is in all things" that is, in all things living. Of course man cannot recapture the spirit as it escapes at death, and once the soul has left the body, it cannot be restored to it again. Only God leads us down to the underworld and up from it again (16:13–14). Thus the author expects the souls of the righteous at least to remain in God's hands (3:1–4). He is sure that when they die the righteous are taken up to God to live with him eternally (4:7–10; 5:5, 15). Man is created for immortality and it is only the ungodly who doubt it (1:13; 2:1, 23).

There is a clear distinction between body and soul as in the current Greek view. The bones will rest in the earth, but the spirit will live (*Jub.* 23:31), for after all it is the image of God on loan from him (*Phocylides* 105–108). By the same token the spirits of the righteous will enter into peace and glory, while the wicked go to the underworld (*Eth. Enoch* 103:4; 108:11). There are even pictures of treasure houses with compartments for the just, for sinners, and for special cases, for "spirits and souls" awaiting judgment (22:3–13). A similar picture is found in 2 Esdras 7:80–87 and *Syriac Baruch* 21:23; 30:2. Josephus puts it in terms that sound even more Greek: In death the soul is freed from the body (*Ant.* 19. 325; *War* 2. 154–55; 6.47; similarly 2 Esdras 7:78, 100).

RESURRECTION

But resistance against taking over Greek ideas as they stood also emerges at this time. Even the Book of Wisdom, which believes that the spirit continued to live after death free from physical bonds, the view held by its Greek contemporaries, still quotes the Old Testament (1 Sam. 2:6) assertion that only God can bring down to Sheol and bring up from there again (16:13). However modern he was in his thinking and however receptive he may have been to Greek thought, the Jew of those days agreed with the Old Testament on the crucial importance of the fact that all life, especially the life in God's eternity after death, is the gift of the Creator, not something automatic, not just a human possession.

In Daniel 12:1–3 we find the first explicit teaching of a resurrection, a resurrection for judgment, for eternal life or eternal damnation. Occasionally we even hear that the earth will keep its dead until they rise again, looking exactly like they did when they died (*Syr. Bar.* 50:2). This is how most Jewish teachers solved the problem, as well as those writers who dealt specifically with the end of the world. After death the "spirit" continued to live on; it would be reunited with the body, however, only at the resurrection, when both would undergo judgment.

One thing however remains unclear. Is the dead body simply reunited with the spirit or will the Spirit of God be given to the body anew?[9]

What Does This Mean?

Through the centuries, Israel had experienced the Spirit of God at work and had attempted to put these experiences into words. From the very beginning the important thing was that

God could break in unexpectedly and destroy all man's thoughts and plans. This is how the prophets and leaders of the people in particular had experienced him, especially in times of crisis. But of course there were also false prophets and false leaders who led the people astray.

By the time of Jesus two points had become clear. On the one hand all spiritual experiences had to be gauged by the lessons Israel had learned over the centuries and by the traditions of the Bible, though of course the Jews did not limit themselves to supposing that God could not work in any way other than through Holy Scripture. On the other hand it is no doubt important to see that human wishes and desires do not get mixed in. But that must not be turned into a theory of inspiration described precisely in psychological terms, as though human reason were eliminated altogether and only God's voice were audible, a theory in which the possibility of all too human voices rising up from the subconscious is excluded.

It remains important that the power of the Spirit is all-embracing. God's Spirit is not simply one force among many. That is why Israel to begin with unquestioningly accepted misfortune, indeed all evil, as the work of God and his Spirit. But gradually it learned to draw clearer distinctions. Of course people could not speak of an evil spirit standing as an equal, side by side with the good Spirit of God, unless they were prepared to surrender all the insights of the Old Testament. But they perceived ever more clearly that man brought about evil by resisting God's laws. Sometimes they felt evil came upon them like an irresistible power. In any case it would be wrong to minimize the power of evil. This insight is expressed in the proliferation of various symbols, such as evil spirits, or even Satan himself. On the other hand not all evil could be blamed on the evil powers. For here too there is something arising from the depth of the human heart, opposing the Spirit of God.

It is clearly impossible to limit the work of the Spirit to the experiences of the prophets, extraordinary as they were, sometimes unique. In the last resort all life must be traced back to the Spirit, including nature with all its fascinating variety and all its glory, as well as our own human senses and faculties.

When everything is attributed to angelic powers, this notion is underscored with particular force. Where people think in more modern and scientific terms, they stress that the Spirit of God is all-embracing, and that it is his function to sustain life. But they do not try to reconcile this with the special utterances of the Holy Spirit, as for instance in the prophets.

Thus the most difficult question is how man participates in the Spirit. Above all, there is no consensus as to whether the whole of creation, including man in his entirety, can be brought into direct connection with the Spirit of God, or whether "flesh" and "spirit" should not rather be divided, "flesh" being construed not only in the Old Testament sense as corruptible and finite in comparison with God and his Spirit but also as earthly and evil over against the divine and good. But even here the resistance of the Jew, influenced as he is by the Old Testament, is discernible. Admittedly, he now talks a lot about the "spirit" as God's highest gift to man. Here he differs from the Old Testament, where man is always a unity, though viewed under different aspects. When man is described in the Old Testament as alive with "spirit" or as perishable with "flesh," this did not mean man's brain or mind as distinct from his bones. All this is now changed under Greek influence. But the Jews still hold fast to the belief that where the spirit leads to true wisdom it is a special gift of God, something added to the purely biological and natural constitution of man.

This becomes particularly important when contemplating the fate of the individual after death. Of course it is still believed that the "spirit" escapes from the corpse and continues to exist in the air or in the underworld or in the heavenly chambers, but people also believe that such a survival is not the complete fulfillment of human destiny. God alone will grant that, and then in such a way that the body too will again receive its due, though in a much more glorious form.

Such are the insights and questions Jesus is faced with during his ministry in Palestine. To that ministry we now turn in the succeeding chapter.

4

The Holy Spirit in the New Testament

Like their Jewish counterparts, the early Christians experienced the work of the Spirit long before they reflected about it and tried to describe it in words. They too learned one lesson at a time; they did not discover right away all the dimensions of the Holy Spirit. If you want to make someone's acquaintance you have to see his entire life, the trivial as well as the important things, his mistakes and his insights, his failures and his successes. It is impossible to be content with a few bare dates and the "results," his final achievements. Thus we must follow step by step the discoveries of the New Testament community and examine all that they experienced with the Holy Spirit.

The Holy Spirit as the Stranger

JESUS

The Sources

The Gospels were written some thirty to seventy years after the death of Jesus. It is obvious even from a cursory reading how different the first three are from the fourth. In them we read mainly individual sayings of Jesus or short speeches. But we notice that Matthew, for example, makes long and connected speeches out of passages which in Mark and Luke were still short and separate. In John on the other hand we find discourses dealing not with the kingdom of God but almost exclusively with the person of Jesus. When Jesus speaks in the synoptists it is in relatively short parables about the kingdom of God. In John by contrast all the figurative language is about Jesus himself. Jesus does not compare himself with this or that, but asserts: "I am the *true* vine, the *good* shepherd, the *true* bread of life." It is impossible that Jesus used both forms of speech, or even that the synoptists preserved one type and John the other. If we ask how Jesus himself spoke we must stay with the first three Gospels and consider each in turn to see how far they expressed in their own language what Jesus said or how far they supplemented it with their editorial comments. Such editing and supplementing was bound to happen; it was only natural. If we repeat someone else's speech or sermon we do the same thing. In the first place we can only tell an experience or event in the way we have experienced it ourselves, and by so doing we sometimes emphasize unimportant items and miss the important ones. This does not mean that John with his entirely different way of reproducing the story is any less true. In certain points he seems to have understood more clearly than the others what Jesus really wanted to say or to express by his actions. But John couches it in his own language and in the language of his times. There are also traces of what Jesus means for the community following his resurrection, and how he dealt with that community. Mark probably offers the oldest written account, while Matthew and Luke use other traditions alongside of Mark.

God Beyond Our Control: The Messiah

The first point we make is a surprising one: Jesus hardly ever spoke about the Spirit. And yet this is not really surprising, for Jesus never presented any actual teaching about God either; instead he nearly always spoke about God in parables. We search equally in vain for any actual teaching about the Christ. Jesus never called himself the Christ (Messiah), the Son of God or Servant of God. Yet throughout his proclamation and especially in his behavior Jesus witnessed to nothing else but God. He did this in a way which far exceeded everything expected from the Messiah, the Son of God or Servant of God. He healed the sick, he called men to be his disciples, and explained that their temporal and eternal salvation depended on whether or not they listened to him (Mark 1:16-34). He forgave sins, often without saying even a word, for example, by calling the tax collectors to eat with him (2:7-17). He never used the formula by which the prophets introduced their message, "Thus says the Lord"; still less did he use that of the theologians, "Thus it is written." His formula instead is: "I say to you," and by it he sets himself in opposition to the Commandment of God (Matt. 5:21–48). Jesus declares openly that in himself, in his own works and proclamation, God's kingdom has already come; he is something like "the finger of God" (Luke 11:20; 17:20–21). Jesus dares, as no Jew had ever dared before, to pray "Abba, Father" (Mark 14:36), and always to speak either of "my Father" or of "your Father." He obviously knows that he stands in a unique relationship to God, that of a son. Hence he can also speak of "Father" and "Son" (Mark 13:32; Matt. 11:27). This of course is not the same as speaking simply of the "Son of God." Whoever speaks like Jesus underscores rather the Son's submission to the "Father," whereas he who speaks of the "Son of God" is stressing that the sonship has reference not to human parents but to God himself, though this of course is not to exclude Jesus' unique relationship with the Father. And finally Jesus endures suffering in a state of loneliness and dereliction such as had never been expected of the Servant of God. He was not some heroic figure admired by his followers, nor was the secret relationship he enjoyed with God an insurance against all pain and agony. In fact, he died with a cry of despair on his lips.

Thus Jesus lives as the Messiah, as the Son of God and God's Servant, and is certainly conscious of it. But he does not deliver any doctrine about it. Instead he points to it by his general demeanor and by the claim of his proclamation, not by any direct formulation.[1]

God Beyond Our Control: The Spirit

The same is true of the Spirit. If what we mean by Holy Spirit is that God is present and active on earth, then all Jesus' works are nothing else but the life of the Spirit of God. But the fact that Jesus does not speak *about* the Spirit but rather acts and speaks *in* the Spirit points to something crucial. In the work of the Spirit we once more encounter God in the first place as a stranger, the unexpected One, the One who cannot immediately be pinned down in an intelligible doctrine. Jesus' appearing on the scene must have been much more shocking than we usually picture it. The way he begins his ministry with a sojourn of forty days in the wilderness has reminded missionaries of certain prophets in Ghana who run into the bush in a sort of ecstasy and disappear there for weeks on end.[2] Then he simply snatches men away from their families and their work; he even speaks of his own mother as if he wanted to have nothing to do with her. He lives off the generosity of the people and sends out his disciples, who in their trades and offices had previously worked as responsible breadwinners for their families, to do his bidding without provisions, money, or cloak. He gets involved with the demon-possessed and breaks the Sabbath. He refuses to throw in his lot with the Zealots who with burning courage and appealing only to the Spirit's exploits in the Old Testament take up what from a human point of view was a hopeless struggle with the Romans. Nor does he take sides with the Sadducees who stood for political restraint, or with the Pharisees who concentrated on individual piety and left politics to its own devices. He bursts suddenly into cries of jubilation and appeals to divine revelations that contradict what God had said in Holy Writ. He befriends people who have not been to synagogue for years and invites prostitutes to eat with him.

Still more important is the way he speaks of God. He tells parables. You can only understand a parable if you allow it to have its effect on you. It may say one thing today and another tomorrow. A parable is never an assured possession. Of course you can memorize it and in that sense appropriate it. But you can never foresee what it might mean in any given situation. When Jesus speaks about God in parables, he does so because God is for him a living God who speaks to us ever anew and whom we can never have at our disposal. We can also say that God's presence in our world is never fixed but always surprising and strange, taking the form of the Holy Spirit, who repeatedly and effectively moves us toward his goals. Where Jesus speaks without parables he usually does so only when he wants to challenge us to some specific action. But even there he offers no cut and dried system which we can take over directly, always assuming that we know what God wants us to do and can act accordingly. The man who wants to tarry to bury his father is told he must come at once (Luke 9:59–62). The other man who wants to follow is sent back home (Mark 5:19). One is asked to give up all his worldly goods (Mark 10:21). Others Jesus visits without expecting them to give away their homes or property (Luke 10:38; Mark 2:15). Even here Jesus offers clear indications of the way we should go and gives us guidelines to prevent us from going wrong. But he gives no universally valid rules to settle every detail. There is only the living God who on each occasion demands anew from us what needs to be done at the moment.

Therefore it is impossible "to own God outright." We have God only as he becomes real for us, only as he becomes a reality that moves and directs us, making us happy and free and causing us to speak and to act. Is that any different from what the Old Testament described? There too God comes upon us as a stranger. He cannot simply be found in the heights of human thinking or in the depths of human psychology. There is nothing there to explain how a man could fall naked to the ground or kill a thousand Philistines. Such things as these show that we never hold God in our power. He destines our lives in complete freedom and yet remains true to himself, not appearing like a will-o'-the-wisp, first here and then there. That means, God comes to us as the Holy Spirit.

What characterizes Jesus is therefore basically quite simple. He really counts on God, and therefore expects that when he tells his parables, in fact in all his activity, in his suffering and dying, that this same living and real God is bearing witness to himself and beginning to act and to speak in person. Apparently the best way to teach about the Holy Spirit is simply to count on him, and without saying too much about him simply let the Spirit permeate one's life.[3]

THE CHURCH'S TEACHING
ABOUT JESUS

Jesus as the Bearer of the Spirit

The strangeness of God and his uncontrollable nature is first expressed in the reluctance of the earliest Gospels to speak of the

presence of God's Spirit in the disciples. In Jesus, and only in
him, has God entered their lives. Hence Jesus is the bearer of
God's Spirit. This corresponds perfectly with Old Testament
thinking, where the Spirit — insofar as he is more than ordinary
vitality — lives only in specially chosen people like the prophets;
only in the end will he be poured out, once and for all, upon all
mankind. The hard saying about the sin against the Holy Ghost
in Mark 3:30 refers to those who refuse to recognize the work of
the Spirit in Jesus' miracles. We cannot go into this verse in detail
here, but it does need to be said that it is not directed against
those who are afraid they might have inadvertently committed
this particular sin. Rather it is spoken against those who, fully
convinced of their own mission, deliberately oppose God,
completely aware of what they are doing. The dire threat of
judgment is therefore aimed at figures who like the Antichrist
want to put themselves in the place of God (see p. 59). We have
already mentioned the saying of Jesus: "If it is by the finger of
God that I cast out demons, then the kingdom of God has come
upon you" (Luke 11:20). Matthew (12:28) replaces "finger of
God" with "Holy Spirit" because he recognizes in Jesus' casting
out of demons the work of the Spirit (cf. also 12:18).

When the three Gospels mention "unclean, evil, or demonic
spirits," as they often do (such language is otherwise found only
in Rev. 16:13–14; 18:2 and in Acts) it is to indicate the
superhuman power which God's Spirit, acting in and through
Jesus, goes out to combat and ultimately to conquer. Where
these spirits get their power from is not a matter for reflection.
Evil is not explained; it is overcome — a view that corresponds by
and large to the belief generally held in contemporary Judaism.
The fact that the Spirit drives Jesus (literally "throws him out")
into combat with the tempter in the wilderness reminds us of
what happened to the prophets (Mark 1:12). Luke emphasizes
more strongly in this passage that Jesus is Lord of the Spirit:
"And Jesus, full of the Holy Spirit, returned . . . and was led by
the Spirit" (4:1). Similarly, we read in Luke 4:14 that it was "in
the power of the Spirit" that Jesus returned to Galilee. Im-
portantly, only Luke gives us, in 4:18, the text of the first
programmatic sermon Jesus preached: "The Spirit of the Lord is

upon me" (Isa. 61:1); in 10:21 Luke speaks of Jesus' rejoicing "in the Spirit." Jesus is the focal point of all these passages. Only in him do the experiences of the Old Testament prophets come alive again. In him the Spirit of God becomes a reality.

This comes out most strongly in the story of Jesus' baptism. Mark 1:10–11 tells us that Jesus saw the heavens opened and the Spirit descend upon him, and that he heard God's voice say to him: "You are my beloved Son . . . ." Mark thus relates it as a vision of Jesus. The later evangelists speak of it more objectively, saying simply that the heavens opened and the Spirit descended. Also, the word from God is expressed in the third person, not addressed to Jesus: "This is my beloved Son." But whether it was Jesus only or others as well who heard and saw it, there can be no doubt that the three evangelists are trying to tell us that the Holy Spirit which descended upon Jesus will be manifested in all his life to come.

Jesus as the Judge and the One who Baptizes in the Spirit

A clear distinction is drawn between Jesus and John the Baptist: John baptizes with water, Jesus with "the Holy Spirit and with fire" (Mark 3:11). Fire is the symbol of judgment, which devours everything that cannot stand before God. We are reminded that "spirit" and "wind" are identical in the Old Testament and that Israel often perceived God's Spirit in the desert wind. In the "wind and fire" God's judgment is present; Jerusalem is punished "with thunder and with earthquake and great noise" (Isa. 29:6):

> Behold, the name of the Lord comes from far,
>   burning earth with his anger . . .
> . . . .
> and his tongue is like a devouring fire.
> (Isa. 30:27–28)

When the "hand of the Lord" comes upon Ezekiel (Ezek. 1:3) the prophet sees a stormy wind coming out of the north, accompanied by a cloud and a flashing fire. A Jewish document from the end of the first century A.D. describes the Son of man from whose mouth comes forth a stream of fire and a storm of sparks (2 Esd. 13:10, 27). Jewish sages describe the last judgment, in terms derived from Malachi 4:1 and Isaiah 41:16, as "fire and storm" (Strack-Billerbeck 4, 853). The same simile is used as in Matthew 3:12: When the grain is threshed, the stormy wind blows all the chaff away. So the word of the Baptist originally heralded the messianic judge who will come with fire and stormy wind. But the church understood that there is nothing so salvific as this judgment that came upon them in Jesus. Thus they learned to understand it as God's holy and sanctifying Spirit. In other words, at the very point at which man understands that his life depends upon God and that he cannot deal with it on his own, Jesus has arrived with his word, and with it something of the Holy Spirit.

The Virgin Birth

This peculiar consciousness of being filled by the Holy Spirit is still more evident in the story of the Virgin Birth. True, Luke tells us (1:15–17) that John the Baptist was filled with the Holy Spirit from the womb, so that he might come "in the spirit and power of Elijah." But what Luke says about Jesus goes much further: Jesus is actually conceived through the Holy Spirit (1:35), and we read very much the same thing in Matthew 1:18. That is why Luke can speak of the Baptist, but not Jesus, becoming strong in spirit (1:80), although what he does say about Jesus otherwise (2:40) sounds pretty much the same.

Now we find it particularly difficult to believe the story of the Virgin Birth. But what does believing it really mean? The important thing is not that we should take it as a biological fact, for this sort of thing was widely believed of other famous men, like Plato or Alexander the Great. They too were believed to have been conceived without a human father. About forty or fifty years later a pagan writer maintains that the Egyptians believed it possible for the spirit of a god to approach a human woman and create life within her. This is for instance the way the hero Heracles was supposed to have been born (Plutarch, *Numa* 4:4 ff.) A virgin birth was something extraordinary according to accepted belief, but it was not unique. So the Virgin Birth does not make Jesus any more than a great man, certainly not the unique Son of God. That was not the novelty which the faith demanded: acceptance of the Virgin Birth as a biological possibility. Such a consideration would have been important only if the flesh, that is, the physical body and its sexuality, were regarded as evil. But such a view would be quite unbiblical. Where that idea is accepted, the logical consequence would be the doctrine of the immaculate conception of Mary. This is the doctrine that, although in the case of Mary's parents there was a sexual act, Mary herself was conceived without sin. But if we agree with the Bible that God is the creator of body and soul, physical frame and (human) "spirit," his free creative activity embraces both. This, then, is the real meaning of the story of the Virgin Birth, and perhaps also of the modern Roman Catholic doctrine of the immaculate conception of Mary: God's free, creative activity, which had always presided over the history of Israel (including therefore the parents of Jesus), came to a head in the birth of Jesus. In biological terms this can take place just as well in the bodily union of two human beings (which in any case must be assumed for the parents of Mary) as without it.

Either way, the Virgin Birth does not play a major role in the New Testament. It appears in none of the various creedal forms, in fact nowhere outside of the two passages mentioned above. Neither does it appear anywhere else in the Gospels of Matthew and Luke, not even in the Christmas story itself. Paul and John knew nothing of it. Paul calls Jesus simply one "born of woman" (Gal. 4:4), which is the way people spoke of everyone at that time. John describes not Jesus but the believers as those "who were born, not of blood nor of the will of the flesh nor of the will of man, but of God" (1:13). Nor does he correct the Jews when they speak of "his father and mother" (6:42). The story is therefore an ambiguous sign that over Jesus' birth there hovers a direct act of the Creator himself such as never happened before in the case of any other human being.

Certainly the Holy Spirit is not involved in any sexual relationship between God and a human being. It is the Spirit of God's creative power as in Genesis 1:2, once more at work at the beginning of the new creation. That is why the giving of the name is much more important for Matthew: "He will save his people from their sins" (1:21–23). For Luke, on the other hand, the important point is Jesus' absolute unity with God, far exceeding that of John the Baptist.[4] It is not the virgin birth of Jesus, but his name and his absolute superiority even over the Baptist that show his unique status. Even if there is more emphasis than at the Baptism that Jesus is the Son of God from the very beginning, what remains supremely important is that God, in his free, underivative action, causes Jesus to be born, who, entirely under the control of his Spirit, will accomplish the saving presence of God. With the affirmation of the Spirit's activity in the birth of Jesus, the mystery of his person is described, though not explained or made intelligible, in a miracle (which was by no means unique by the standards of the day).

The Spirit as the Power of
Jesus' Resurrection

This realization eventually led to the post-Easter understanding of the resurrection as the work of the creative Spirit of God. In Romans 1:3–4 Paul cites a primitive confession of the community which states that Jesus was "born from David according to the flesh and installed as Son of God according to the Spirit of holiness by the power of his resurrection from the dead" [author's version]. This is still in conformity with Old Testament thought. As we are constantly asked in school: "What is this — for example, what type of plant, what geological stratum, what verb tense?" so there is only one question a child of Israel was always asked in Old Testament days: "What happened next?" This is because the most important lesson a child had to learn was the story of the acts of God in Israel. For the ancient Israelite did not think in abstract terms as we do, wondering whether a person might be a king or son of God. What did interest him was whether that person "functioned" as such, for example, whether he might reign as son of God in God's stead. Thus, according to Psalm 2:7, God could say to the king at his accession: "You are my son, / today I have begotten you," since it was on this day of coronation that the king began to reign in God's stead.

Again, the New Testament community did not begin by

asking whether or not Jesus is *in himself* the Son of God but rather whether he reigned over them as God's Son. Thus it was in this sense that they viewed the exaltation of Jesus after his resurrection as the moment when he began to reign over them in heaven. And they understood this as the act of God's Spirit. Others adopted a different view, identifying his baptism or his birth with the inauguration of his activity as Son of God.[5] Similarly, a primitive hymn asserts of Jesus: "He was manifested in the flesh / vindicated in the Spirit" (who raised him and gave him a part in God's reign, 1 Tim. 3:16). Then there is the formula in 1 Peter 3:18, which says that Jesus was "put to death in the flesh, but was made alive in the spirit." Paul too says that the Spirit of him who raised Jesus from the dead dwells in the faithful (see p. 111).

The Meaning of These Passages

All these passages except the last are really speaking not so much about the Spirit as about Jesus. They do not actually attempt to give a precise explanation of why Jesus was able to do the things he did. On the contrary, all these statements about the Spirit of God are attempts to underscore the inexplicable element in the activity of Jesus. The fact that the Spirit of God was at work in him is what raised Jesus above everything that was human or capable of human explanation. This shows how amazed the early community is at the miracle of the renewed activity of the presence of God. Thus it experiences the reality of God in the first place as opposition to all evil in the world of man: The Spirit of God leads Jesus into battle against the Tempter in the desert; he casts out the "evil spirit" and heals the possessed. In him the storm of God's judgment comes down upon every obstacle in the way of the coming kingdom, bringing salvation to all who are ready to accept that judgment. In this sense the Spirit of God presides over the whole life of Jesus and shows him to be the beloved Son from the moment of his baptism. Only from him does man learn something of this divine reality that comes alive in the Spirit.

This unique oneness with the Spirit of God assumes concrete shape in the story of the Virgin Birth, and Luke gives it even greater precision by making Jesus superior to the Baptist with respect to his endowment with the Spirit. That is why Luke speaks of Jesus acting "in the Spirit" in various ways, unlike other evangelists before him who said that the Spirit drove him. Luke deliberately seeks to emphasize Jesus' actions and to differentiate Jesus, as the unique bearer of the Spirit, from all Old Testament and other contemporary prophets who could be bounced about—almost like a ball—by some inexplicable power. The Spirit is precisely not a superhuman power, which would more or less exclude any initiative on the part of Jesus. Jesus himself, all that he says and does, is God's presence. In him the age of God's salvation is dawning. His life and proclamation is the event of God's presence, fulfilling all prophetic expectations. That is the life of the Holy Spirit.

For this reason Luke conceives the action of the Spirit in Jesus primarily as the power behind Jesus' proclamation of the gospel (4:18, 14–15), which power subsequently continues in his disciples (12:12). In this sense Luke goes beyond his predecessors. In what he says about the Spirit Luke does not merely attempt to convey that Jesus is unique; Jesus is not just One who goes beyond the prophets of old, even though his experience of the Spirit is like theirs. Luke wants to say something more. The time has begun which was expected by the prophets; Jesus is the One in whom what the prophets prophesied has become a present reality. Thus we can feel how the evangelists strove to give clear expression to this mystery. Even before them the community had ascribed to the Spirit that which distinguished Jesus from all other men, even the greatest of the prophets. His resurrection from the dead had made him Lord of the community. He was from then on its head and ruler. We must now turn our attention to that.

THE "ALIEN" SPIRIT IN THE
LIFE OF THE COMMUNITY

The First Three Gospels

The Baptist's saying about the coming of the judge (Matt. 3:10–12) was so important to the evangelists that they used it to preface their account of the work of Jesus. This shows how profound was their experience of the pervasive work of the Spirit against all opposition, and as a bulwark against all their own misplaced endeavors.

Two further passages in the Gospels deal with this. First, there is Mark 13:11 (cf. Luke 12:11–12). This passage promises the disciples that when they are brought to trial because of their faith the Holy Spirit will stand by their side and tell them what they are to say. There is no need for them to meditate about it beforehand. This agrees with the Old Testament. The Spirit would help them in moments of exceptional perplexity. That help would come as a kind of prophetic intuition. Luke reproduces this saying in the same context as Mark 13:11. The (risen) Jesus himself will give his disciples the right word to say (Luke 21:14–15). Luke intends to emphasize that the Spirit is no other than the Spirit of Jesus himself (cf. pp. 51–52).

The second passage is Mark 14:38. The Spirit will help in the battle against a world at enmity with God. Yet this world lives on even in the believer in the form of temptation. The believer needs the help of the Spirit not only in exceptional cases, as when he is brought before a court of law, but at all times: "Watch and pray that you may not enter into temptation; the spirit indeed is willing, but the flesh is weak." The clue to this saying lies in Psalm 51:12, where the "willing spirit" is none other than the God-given "holy Spirit" of verse 11 (cf. p. 26). Here the New Testament latches on to the Old. It is especially in the battle against temptation, that is, for his life on this earth, that the disciple of Jesus is promised the help of the Spirit, not only for rare moments but for all times.

The Acts of the Apostles: Miracles

Miracles are important for Luke. He even narrates healings performed by Peter's shadow and by handkerchiefs which had been in contact with Paul (Acts 5:15–16; 19:12). This sounds like the worst kind of superstition. But it is noticeable that Luke always speaks of the "power" of God in such cases. Of course, it is true that "power" and "Spirit" are closely related. The Spirit is certainly the "power from on high" (Luke 24:49; cf. also 1:17, 35;

4:14). Yet Luke consistently distinguishes between the two. In connection with miracles he always speaks of the "power" of God rather than the "Spirit" of God. He obviously does not wish to connect the activity of the Holy Spirit too closely with the working of miracles. That is why he no longer follows Mark in identifying the sin against the Holy Spirit with the rejection of Jesus' exorcisms; for Luke it is rather a refusal to bear witness to Jesus (Luke 12:10–12). Similarly, in the Beelzebub controversy he still uses the old-fashioned phrase, "finger of God," while Matthew speaks of the Holy Spirit (Luke 11:20). Probably Luke is a little uncomfortable if the working of miracles is too closely connected with the Holy Spirit. It is true that in his action upon man the Spirit descends even to the level of the body. But he cannot be directly grasped. You cannot regard every miracle as unquestionably the work of the Spirit. The Spirit is experienced in the first place where there is a word pointing unequivocally to Christ. Miraculous healings and similar phenomena could come from entirely different "power," even powers opposed to God (10:19). That is why miracles must be done explicitly in the name of Jesus (Acts 4:30, 9:34; 16:18; 19:13).

Perhaps nowadays we should put it like this: it is quite probable that man has mysterious God-given powers. For instance, there is the power of suggestion or acupuncture or the skills of medicine men in Africa. Modern man has for the most part lost these powers. They are not supernatural but gifts of God's creation and in this sense works of his Spirit. But the question is, how is one to interpret these powers? Are they really gifts of the Spirit? Perhaps the one exercising the powers does not think about it at all. Perhaps he deliberately seeks to use them against God. They are therefore very similar to all the other powers available to man, like his reason or artistic ability. What started out as a gift from God may be used without a thought for the Giver. Or the gifts may be misused so as to have the very oposite effect to what God intended. In point of fact we might say that there is only one miracle of the Holy Spirit, God's word to us, which is always a word of love, whether it comes in "normal" or "abnormal" ways (see p. 94). That is why Luke speaks of the Holy Spirit only when this supreme miracle occurs.

Of course he knows that the healing of disease or a prophecy of things to come through which God tries to speak to us, occur through the "power" of God or of the Spirit (cf. pp. 75–78). This shows that the only place it is possible to speak unambiguously of the works of God is where there has been not only a physical healing but where a person has also been led by the word of proclamation to Jesus himself. Luke emphasized this in the story of the ten lepers. What is normally said to everyone healed is here said only to one, the one who returned to give thanks to God: "Your faith has made you well" (Luke 17:19).

The Acts of the Apostles:
Speaking in Tongues and Prophecy

Just as the people said of the prophet, "The man of the spirit is mad" (Hos. 9:7), so they said of the apostles on the day of Pentecost, "They are filled with new wine" (Acts 2:3). That is what the event of Pentecost looked like. It started with a strange noise: there was a sound like the rushing of a mighty wind. There were tongues of fire like lightning (vv. 2–3). Even stranger, however, was the sequel: they all began to speak and complete chaos ensued. Nobody would normally have understood a thing. But the story takes an even stranger turn. A multitude of Jews, of different languages, understood what the apostles were saying, every one in his own language (v.8)! We cannot tell at this distance what exactly happened. Was it just the eleven apostles (without Judas) who spoke, or the hundred and twenty faithful (1:15)? What kind of "house" was it? Were they inside or in front of it? For we are told that many thousands (v. 41) could hear what was going on. How are we to explain all those languages? There were no longer any Medes or Elamites by that time (v. 9). And how were all those languages represented among "Jews dwelling in Jerusalem" (v. 5)? They would in any case all have spoken Aramaic or at least Greek, even if they had previously lived in other countries. They would hardly have learned the local dialects but only Greek or Latin, which was spoken everywhere. Or perhaps they were just casual visitors to the festival and maybe Luke writes in this vein because Pentecost was already known in the Greek Bible as the "feast of the church" (Deut. 4:10; 9:10; 18:16) and was regarded as the day of the Law-giving (*Jub.* 1:1; 6:17-19; 15:1). For this is how the giving of the Law at Sinai was pictured in those days: God's voice came down in the form of a flame and blew like a "spirit" through the trumpets so that their echo reached to the ends of the earth (Philo, *On the Decalogue* 33, *On the Special Laws* 2. 189). Perhaps Luke wished to say that God was repeating at Pentecost what he had first done on Sinai when he gave the ten commandments to Israel. If Luke had this story before him as he wrote, all the details fall into place. Or perhaps Luke is thinking of the divisions of the tower of Babel being overcome (Gen. 11:9), and that is why understanding of the various languages was so important.

But the main question is this: Does Luke really believe in a miraculous gift of languages? How could such a thing be conceived? If every apostle spoke another tongue, there would have to be an additional miracle in order for him to be heard above the chaos. Or did Luke think of it rather as a miracle of hearing? Were they supernatural "tongues of angels" (1 Cor. 13:1), understood by everyone in his mother tongue? The whole thing remains a mystery. Obviously the narrator does not want us to get bogged down with the details so long as we realize that something happened which healed the divisions of the tower of Babel. This was something even greater than what God did for Israel at Sinai. Of course Luke is describing in this story how the Spirit of God broke into the community in a strange and surprising way. And he was right about that from a historical point of view. The Jerusalem community must have experienced from the beginning the new irruption of the Spirit, for all the remarkable prophets whom Luke still knows by name come from Jerusalem (Acts 11:27-28; 15:32; 20:8-11) and some at least of those mentioned in 13:1 are originally from Palestine. In some respects these prophets are like Old Testament figures. They predict the future (cf. 20:23; 21:4). Sometimes they perform symbolic actions; for example, the prophet binds his own hands and feet with Paul's girdle (21:11). Unlike Paul, Luke seems to regard this "prophesying" (or prediction) as identical with "speaking in tongues" (19:6). This makes the quotation from Joel (which speaks of the prophecy) suitable for the speaking of tongues at Pentecost (2:17), and it was probably Luke himself, going beyond the Old Testament, who was responsible for adding the reference to prophecy in verse 18.

The gift of tongues or foreign languages is not confined to Jerusalem (cf. also pp. 90–93). It is also given to Gentiles at Caesarea and to the disciples of the Baptist at Ephesus (Acts 10:47; 11:15, 17; 8:19, 6), although nothing is said about their speaking in foreign languages or their being understood by people of foreign tongues. This aspect of the matter does not seem to be important to Luke apart from its similarity to the stories of the tower of Babel and Sinai. That should serve as a warning to us not to attach too much importance to it when it occurs nowadays.

The Acts of the Apostles:
The Baptism of the Spirit

The granting of the Holy Spirit means for Luke the fulfillment of John the Baptist's prophecy. John baptized with water but the One who is to come would baptize with the Holy Spirit. Jesus himself repeats this prophecy in Acts 1:5 and Peter reminds us of it in Acts 11:16. But neither passage refers to the baptism of fire which John the Baptist tied in with it (Luke 3:16). Although Luke mentions the flames of fire at Pentecost he does not seem to regard this as the fulfillment of John the Baptist's saying. It is only an accompanying phenomenon pointing to the extraordinary manner in which the Spirit of God would irrupt. This means that the flames at Pentecost were not themselves the fire of judgment of which John the Baptist had spoken earlier. Moreover, Luke takes it for granted that all converts after Pentecost were also baptized with water. Is it possible to distinguish between Spirit baptism and water baptism?

The narrative of Acts does not fit into any neat pattern. The Spirit comes upon the apostles and the small group of faithful who were with them without any mention of a water baptism either before or after (Acts 2:1–11). The Spirit of God also comes to Cornelius and his family. At first Peter is afraid to baptize them with water. But subsequently he relents and baptizes them with water after all. The Samaritans are baptized with water to be sure, but they receive the Spirit only later through the apostles (8:14–17). The disciples at Ephesus have received the baptism of water from John but must now be baptized again with water in the name of Jesus, and this time receive the Holy Spirit when Paul lays hands upon them (19:2–6). Paul is baptized by an ordinary member of the community. The laying on of hands restores his eyesight, which he lost when the risen One appeared to him. He is promised the gift of the Holy Spirit, but the narrative tells us only that he submitted to baptism. This is probably because the gift of the Spirit is considered as a matter of course to be a part of baptism. This is the way it is in 2:38, where Peter promises all the converts that they would receive the Holy Spirit if they submit to baptism. The same is probably true wherever reference is made to (water) baptism but not to a Spirit baptism distinct from it (2:41; 8:38; 16:15, 33; 18:8; 22:16). In these instances all we hear is that the candidate believed, and was filled with joy. Thus the Spirit blows where he wills and nobody can prescribe where he should appear. As a rule the baptism of water and of the Spirit coincide. Where a person comes to be baptized in faith God gives him the Holy Spirit, and thereby the strength to live in faith. Luke mentions such striking phenomena as speaking in tongues only where it is God's purpose to take some new extraordinary step for his people. This was the case right at the beginning, where God's purpose was to turn the helpless disciples into messengers of the gospel. The same thing happened with the half-pagan Samaritans; it was important then for the church in Jerusalem to recognize what was happening and see the continuity with the saving acts of God. Then there was that question – so important for the future – where even Peter was helpless and unknowing: whether the Gentiles should be accepted and baptized without first having to become Jews and submit to circumcision. Finally there was the problem of the sufficiency of John's baptism, that is, sincere repentance and conversion to the word of God on the Old Testament model. Only in these instances is there any specific mention of the gifts of the Spirit before, at, or after baptism.

Thus it is wrong to say that a person does not really belong to Jesus until some striking phenomenon occurs or until he speaks in tongues. Nor, conversely, can we simply insist on people believing that the Holy Spirit is given in water baptism. The effects may be very divergent. Sometimes there is an earthquake (Acts 4:31), sometimes speaking in tongues in the exuberant joy of faith. But in every case a baptized person himself ought to be able to say whether he has received the Spirit or has still not even heard of such a thing (19:2). But we should not forget that the Spirit can also appear in a quiet and unobtrusive manner (cf. p. 76).

In a church which practices infant baptism the question is more difficult. If the Spirit is, as Luke says (Acts 5:32), mainly the power enabling those who already believe to persevere in faith, then we must attach particular importance to the decision which a baptized person has to make as an adolescent or adult. If the Spirit, as Paul says, gives us receptivity to Jesus before we do anything for God, infant baptism must at the same time be understood as a sign that God has laid his hand upon a person, long before that person decides for God. The danger of infant baptism is that it can be regarded as magic. It is so easy to forget the grave responsibility for Christian living which baptism places upon the baptized infant and his parents. Conversely, the danger of adult baptism lies in the fact that the person baptized may regard his decision for God — sometimes brought about by traditional expectations or by all kinds of psychic pressure — as more important than the baptismal gift itself. There is something to be said for both practices. Even where infant baptism is universally practiced, adult baptism is the norm to begin with, in the mission field at least. And again, where adult baptism is generally practiced at the outset, growing children are generally admitted at an age when they are, for example, not yet capable of making lifelong decisions on matters like career and marriage. So the question is, which is the greater danger at any given time, the almost automatic ritual of baptism where nobody really seriously grasps what he is doing, or the overestimation of personal decision in which the "true church" feels itself superior to the others, while at the same time dictating to the Holy Spirit how the candidate is to be brought to this decision? It cannot be denied that the first danger is rampant in the West today. At least it must be counteracted through very serious and open dialogue with the parents and godparents.

The Epistles of the New Testament and John

It is striking what extraordinary effects the Spirit produces in the Pauline communities: speaking with tongues, healing of the sick, prophecy. Paul in no way denies that these things are gifts of the Spirit. He himself came to them "not only in word, but also in power and in the Holy Spirit" (1 Thess. 1:5; similarly 1 Cor. 2:4; Rom. 15:19, which also speaks of "signs and wonders"). Paul can also remind the church how the Spirit when he comes displays his presence in tangible deeds of power (Gal. 3:2, 5). In his earliest extant letter Paul warns the Thessalonians: "Do not quench the Spirit, do not despise prophesying" (1 Thess. 5:19–20). Thus it seems as if the appearance of the Spirit as manifested in the prophets of the community had made a somewhat uncanny impression upon the Thessalonians. The strangeness of the Spirit is particularly expressed in 1 Corinthians 2:9–16: "What no eye has seen, nor ear heard, / nor the heart of man conceived, / God has revealed to us in the Spirit." The natural [RSV margin] man does not receive the speech [author's translation; RSV gifts; Gr. things] of God, for it is folly to him because it is discerned only in the Spirit [author's translation; RSV spiritually discerned]. Of course this is not simply because the language of the Spirit is strange. It is really the message the Spirit conveys that is strange, the revelation of the Crucified (cf. pp. 78–80).

Finally, the Letter to the Hebrews describes the experiences of those who have come to faith in Jesus: they "have once been enlightened, . . . have tasted the heavenly gift, and have become partakers of the Holy Spirit, and have tasted the good word of God and the powers of the age to come" (6:4–5). Both factors played an important role in the later history of the church. "Illumination" appealed to the Hellenistic church fathers, familiar as they were with Alexandrian philosophy, while endowment with the "power of the age to come" was what mattered in many prophetic movements.[6] The latter applies equally to the understanding of the Spirit in the Book of Revelation. When the prophet John is "in the Spirit" (1:10; 4:2; 17:3; 21:10) he is caught up out of this world, almost as it were "transported," and has a vision of the heavenly world. But the Spirit has something to say in quite a sober way to the everyday life of the community too. This is shown in the letters to the seven churches (chapter 2–3), where the author calls for quite practical decisions, sometimes praising the churches and sometimes rebuking them. Perhaps the most striking passage is John 3:8, where Jesus says that anyone born anew or from above by the Spirit is like the wind that blows where it will: you hear the sound of it but you do not know whence it comes or whither it goes (cf. p. 71).

WHAT DOES THIS MEAN?

Like Israel, the New Testament church experienced in the Spirit the irruption of an alien power. It never got over its amazement that God had become a reality and a presence. It was anything but natural that God should start speaking and acting with human beings. So extraordinary was it at the outset that the only thing the church could say was that the Spirit of God had come alive in Jesus. Jesus had accepted the reality of God in a perfectly natural way. That is why he went ahead so confidently, so bravely, always opening himself to people and events and hearing the call of God in them. Jesus was always ready to break away from convention and the tyranny of fashion, yet at any moment he could see God at work in the most ordinary everyday happenings. He let God be God, never offering any doctrine about him, nor for that matter about the Messiah or about the Spirit either. So the church learned from Jesus himself to take the mystery of God seriously. God is life, and man can experience that life but not package and label it neatly like any ordinary object. When the Old and New Testaments speak of God encountering us in his "living" spirit, what is meant is this activity which is always free, always determined by God himself, and yet never like a will-o'-the-wisp. That is why Luke and Paul, like later witnesses, saw the work of the Spirit in unexpected events, in miracles, in the healing of the sick, and in prophecy. Yet it soon became obvious to all that this was not enough; that would be to confine God once again to a rigid pattern. God can speak to us quite apart from extraordinary phenomena, and conversely, the extraordinary is not necessarily an expression of the special presence of God. Above all, God is to be recognized not by some outward form, however strange, but by *what* he says and *what* he does. As in the Old Testament, God appears as One who is at once beyond our control and who speaks his word with supreme clarity (cf. pp. 22–23), only now this points directly to Jesus. This, too, the New Testament church learned step by step, a matter to which we turn now.

The Holy Spirit in Creation and in the New Creation

THE STATEMENTS ABOUT CREATION

Unlike the Old, the New Testament hardly ever speaks of creation, nor does it ever mention the work of the Spirit in creation. This is because the Old Testament belief in God as Creator of heaven and earth is presupposed and unquestioned. Consequently, the New Testament community does not deny the work of the Creator-Spirit throughout the universe. Its concern is that the Spirit should be recognized and obeyed. Because of this the church confines itself for the most part to the Spirit's effects within its own community, where people try to live the new life in voluntary obedience to the Spirit (Mark 10:42–43). It is not concerned with what can be accomplished through the law—for example, in New Testament times by the authority of the paterfamilias or today by the authority of the state—(see Philem. 14). Jesus himself had spoken of One who clothes lilies of the field more gloriously than King Solomon with all his riches and who feeds the birds that neither sow nor reap nor gather into barns (Matt. 6:26–30), and who also knows about sparrows that fall to the ground—even this cannot happen without the will of the Creator (10:29). But Jesus is not concerned with the doctrine of creation. On the contrary, he takes it for granted that his audience already knows about that. He only reminds them of it in order to give them courage really to believe.

Pretty much the same is true of all the relevant passages in the New Testament. When the first three Gospels tell us that the heavens opened at Jesus' baptism so that God's Spirit could descend (Mark 1:9), and when John emphasizes that the Spirit remained with Jesus (1:33), they understand that, as Jewish writings show, to be the beginning of God's new and final creation. Luke makes Paul in Athens speak explicitly in Old Testament language about creation (Acts 17:24-27). But by doing so he presupposes that all Jews, enlightened pagans, and Christians alike know this, and what he really underscores is the message about Jesus, his resurrection, and the last judgment. Paul refers to him through whom all things exist (1 Cor. 8:6), who calls into existence the things that do not exist (Rom. 4:17), who causes light to shine out of darkness (2 Cor. 4:6). But in all three passages he does so only to speak of God, who said Yes to us in Jesus. This is such a miracle for Paul that he can conceive of it only as a new creation, as an entirely new world which God has prepared for us.

There is one passage where Paul speaks about the creation at greater length (Rom. 8:18-23). But there he is speaking in highly realistic terms about its suffering and groaning. Whole forests are ruined by pests, deer are trapped in the snow and torn apart by foxes, cats catch mice and play with them before killing them, earthquakes lay whole countries to waste—all this is included in a matter of fact way in Paul's general view of nature (cf. p. 109). But again, for Paul it all points to the new creation. This time, however, what he has in mind is the hope of final, new creation. Only then will man be redeemed and the whole created order be taken up into God's good life free from suffering and death.

The hymn quoted in Colossians 1:15-20 goes even further. Unlike Acts, it expresses the belief that we can speak of the creation of God only when we have seen the real face of God in Jesus. Otherwise we have no means of knowing that creation, despite all its menacing, terrifying, and dubious features, is already encompassed by the love of God. When the hymn describes Jesus as the "beginning" of creation, the One in whom all things hold together, it is trying to say that in him there became visible every moment of God's love which was already at work in creation and still pervades the whole of nature. Similarly, Hebrews 1:7 and 10 reminds us of the word of the psalmist: "Who makes his angels winds," who founded the earth in the beginning. But he does this only to emphasize how infinitely superior Jesus is to all the angels.

So nature can indeed point to God. Someone like Francis of Assisi knew this full well. But we must not succumb to romanticism and close our eyes to the terrors and sorrows of nature. We must learn to see them through the eyes of Jesus. Or rather, we must learn from Jesus that God really made his creatures out of love. And they can return that love—even if a sparrow falls to the ground, and people are killed, and even if God's own Son is crucified (Matt. 10:28-29; 16:21). But the problem of evil will be discussed later (see p. 121).

THE NEW CREATION THROUGH
THE SPIRIT: PAUL

Only Matthew among the first three Gospels mentions amongst the sayings of Jesus the "new creation" or "new birth" (19:28). These formulations, which have their parallels in contemporary Jewish thought, probably come from the evangelist himself. Luke 22:30 has a similar saying, though without this particular expression. What the expression means is the final consummation at the end of the world, namely, the universal new creation (see pp. 108-11).

Paul on the other hand calls it a "new creation" when an individual comes to faith (2 Cor. 5:17). Presumably he is referring to more than just that individual's subjective experience. Paul wants to say that this human being is now completely stamped by Christ; he is as it were completely surrounded by Christ and lives "in Christ." In other words, the new creation is this new world into which the believer is admitted. Hence in 1 Corinthians 12:13 Paul can say: "By one Spirit we were all baptized into one body . . . and were all made to drink of one Spirit."

This statement reminds us of those pictures in which the prophets portrayed what the Creator would do on the last day:

> I will pour water on the thirsty land,
> and streams on the dry ground.
>
> (Isa. 44:3; see p. 00)

or

> I give water in the wilderness,
>   rivers in the desert,
> to give drink to my chosen people.
>
> (43:20)

In Jesus therefore a whole new world has come into being. Different laws are now in effect. No longer is there universal strife, each against all, everyone trying to climb higher than everyone else and force as many down below him as he can. This new creation can be realized upon earth only in a very fragmentary way. But how can we believe in complete salvation unless we have at least a glimpse of it here on earth?

Paul can say that the believer is transported into this new world. But he can also say that this new world seeks to penetrate the believer's heart. Without speaking explicitly of the Spirit, Paul can put this thought into the language of creation: "It is the God who said, 'Let light shine out of darkness,' who has shone in our hearts to give the light of the knowledge of the glory of God in the face of Christ" (2 Cor. 4:6). Finally, the Epistle to Titus takes up the same idea when it calls baptism "the washing of regeneration and renewal in the Holy Spirit" (Titus 3:5). This gives us the key word which plays such a big part in the dialogue with Nicodemus (John 3:1-2).

THE NEW CREATION THROUGH
THE SPIRIT: JOHN

The whole dialogue between Jesus and Nicodemus revolves around the question how man can be born "anew," or perhaps more accurately "from above," that is, "by the Spirit" (John 3:3–8). At first glance it looks as if this is simply a way of describing the peculiar experience of the Old Testament prophets: nobody knows whence the man endowed with the

Holy Spirit came nor whither he will go. It sounds like the disciples of Elijah who were afraid that the Spirit of God had taken their master up to a high mountain or thrown him down a deep ravine, no one being able to know what might happen next once a person is under the influence of the Spirit. But we must notice in the passage the close connection between God's work in creation and what he does in the believers: "The wind [RSV margin: Spirit] blows where it wills . . . so it is with everyone who is born of the Spirit." God allows his Spirit to act with sovereign freedom, as in nature so also in the person who opens himself to the guidance of the Spirit. Of course we must speak of the full freedom of God when we speak of the Holy Spirit. But this freedom is not manifested in startling or peculiar happenings. Such a notion never crosses John's mind. The promise that the disciples will do even "greater works" than Jesus himself (John 14:12) is perhaps the only suggestion that they will perform miracles. But if "the work of God" consists in bringing a person to faith (6:29), this promise does not refer to the healing of the sick or comparable activities, but only says that the disciples have the task of calling all nations to faith. Jesus tells Nicodemus the same thing. The new "birth" in the Spirit is the awakening of faith. There are many pagan parallels to such things as healings. Although rare, they are not inexplicable. But for John the supreme miracle is when a person is brought to faith. When that happens a new world dawns, a new kind of life begins. Similarly John 6:63 speaks of the "life-giving Spirit" who gives life to the believers through Jesus' word. Here again it is the Creator-Spirit that summons us into life. What once happened in creation and constantly recurs wherever God creates life, what will happen at the resurrection at the end of time, is the same thing that happens when a person is brought to faith through Jesus' word. And just as the Spirit "makes the winds blow" (Ps. 147:18), so too he causes "streams of living water" to flow forth from Jesus and the believer (John 7:38–39; cf. 4:14). What this means above all is the life-giving proclamation of the Spirit in the disciples (20:22), though that means not just talk but an all-embracing life-style.

The Book of Revelation (thought not of course by the same

author) strongly insists that this Spirit not only moves the individual but is also the creative power of God which builds a new world. This book presents a vivid picture of the seven spirits standing like angels before the throne of God and being sent into all the world to carry out his creative purpose. At the same time they are the "seven eyes" of the "lamb that was slain" (Rev. 4:5; 5:6). God thus transforms this world by looking at it with the eyes of Jesus Christ who has done everything for it. By looking at the world in this way God creates it anew. The author of Revelation takes this so seriously that he actually visualizes the one Spirit of God (2:7 ff.) addressing the seven churches to whom he writes. That is why in speaking of God, and the Spirit, and Jesus Christ, the author says that "the seven Spirits" which come like angels to the seven churches are in Jesus' hand (1:4-5; 3:1; cf. 1:20). Therefore Revelation makes both points: Not only is the Spirit seeking to create a new world, he is also doing it as the Spirit of revelation or prophecy (19:10; 22:6). He calls communities into life and will use them to withstand all the powers of evil. Their cry to Jesus to come and bring an end to wrong and suffering is the cry of the Spirit itself (22:17).

WHAT DOES IT MEAN TO BE BORN AGAIN?

If an obstetrician thought that every childbirth had to be exactly like all the others he would soon lose his license on the grounds of negligent homicide. It is only spiritual midwives who think everyone must be born again in exactly the same way — the way they experienced it themselves. But what Jesus tells us is quite different. He tells us that being born again or from above is a sheer gift. The Spirit blows where it wills, and no one can tell in advance how this will happen. Nicodemus is told only that it does not depend on his own ability, his knowledge of Scripture, or his faith. It depends on whether or not he has been overcome by love: "God so loved the world . . ." (John 3:16). In a remarkable picture Jesus tells Nicodemus he must learn to look to the cross and submit to the victorious power of him who dies there, just as the Israelites, bitten in the wilderness by serpents, had to look for healing to the bronze serpent which Moses had set upon a pole (3:14–15; cf. Num. 21:6–9). This is the way it is. If we can no longer get away from this Jesus who held fast to the bitter end, even to the cross, God has overpowered us and something of this "creation from above" has already taken place. "Everyone who believes that Jesus is the Christ is born of God" (NIV, 1 John 5:1). When that has happened we have come to know God, and from his love are learning to love (1 John 4:7). In fact, we are so completely immersed in our whole life with its ups and downs, its sunshine and its shadows, its blessings and its failures, that John can even say that this is the new righteousness in which we sin no more (1 John 2:29; 3:9; 5:18).

There is no fixed pattern here. Nothing is said of the agony of repentance, nothing of any describable experience of liberation. What we do hear about is that our faith in Jesus is given to us in such a way that some of God's love is kindled in our hearts too. Our whole life is directed toward God and no longer toward all sorts of other things. This experience is a perfectly natural one, even though it is still the miracle of miracles. As Jesus said, we learn to live like the flowers and the birds, opening ourselves up to the Spirit, the same Spirit which is at work in creation and seeks to unite us with the whole choir of creatures praising God. Here John attains an insight which has only gradually become evident to the community. More of this in the next chapter.

The Holy Spirit as the Source of Our Knowledge of God

THE SPIRIT GIVEN TO ALL BELIEVERS

It is true that Luke wrote later than Paul. But the Lucan writings reflect more strongly than Paul's a community faith that has not yet absorbed all the new insights a great teacher such as Paul considered important. John the Baptist had long since foretold One who would baptize with the "Spirit." The church of Jesus understood this to mean the gift of the Spirit which Jesus wills to give to all who turn to him. This is something quite new compared with the Old Testament, where the Spirit is expected to be given to all only at the glorious End (see p. 26). Luke underscores that this has already happened. The little parable of the father who would never give his child a serpent instead of a fish probably ended originally: "How much more will your Father who is in heaven give good things to those who ask him?" (Matt. 7:11). Luke changes this to "give the Holy Spirit," because for him the Holy Spirit is the very gift of God to his church, the one good thing which God gives. We can still see what Luke took this to mean. He attributes the assistance given the disciples before a court of law (Luke 12:12) not only to the Holy Spirit but also to the resurrected Jesus (21:15; see p. 58). The last days announced by the prophets did not occur just once in the first three decades of our era; they are alive in Jesus *and* in his community. That is why Luke attaches so much importance to the fact that it is the resurrected Jesus himself who gives the Spirit to his church (Luke 24:49; Acts 2:23; also John 7:39; 20:22). Luke took it seriously that only in Jesus do we see into the very "heart" of God. This has reference not only to the earthly Jesus, however much his words and deeds help us to understand God; what really matters is that he who lived and died as Jesus now encounters his church as the risen and living One, who in their new situation, as for instance in persecution, opens to them new paths. Again, in his reinterpretation of the saying about the sin against the Holy Ghost (Luke 12:10–11; see p. 59), Luke depicts the Spirit as the One who helps sustain our faith even in the midst of a hostile world.

All this applies equally to Acts. Both Peter (Acts 2:38; 15:8–9) and Paul (19:2) take it for granted that in baptism the believers receive the Holy Spirit. In the Epistles of the New Testament the statement that "to each is given the manifestation of the Spirit for the common good" (1 Cor. 12:7) occurs eight times in a similar form (Rom. 12:3; 1 Cor. 3:5; 7:7, 17; Eph. 4:7; 1 Pet. 4:10). In Romans 8:9 we read: "Anyone who does not have the Spirit of Christ does not belong to him." When our common baptism is referred to as "the washing of regeneration" (Titus 3:5) this means very much the same thing. John 7:39 speaks of "the Spirit, which those who believe in him were to receive." Even the Spirit who grants forgiveness (John 20:22–23) is imparted to all believers. In the farewell discourses the "disciples" (John hardly ever speaks of the "Twelve") represent the future community.

This means that the promise can not be confined to the clergy any more than, for example, the commandment of love in 15:9–17. Finally, the baptized, according to Hebrews 6:4, have become partakers of the Spirit, and in the letters to the seven churches in Revelation 2–3 the Spirit addresses not individuals but the church as a whole. Thus the New Testament is unanimous in recognizing that it is impossible to belong to Jesus without experiencing something of the Holy Spirit. If that is not to remain an illusion, however, we must take very seriously indeed what has just been said: The Spirit *may*, but by no means *must*, be seen in striking phenomena. In what other way then is he to be seen?

THE SPIRIT AS AN AID TO PREACHING THE GOSPEL: LUKE

The Spirit as a Gift for Those Who Already Believe

At the outset the church experienced the Spirit in the extraordinary, just as in the Old Testament. But the church soon learned that, unlike the way it was in the Old Testament, the Spirit is given to all believers. True, the church did not immediately attribute its faith to the work of the Spirit, but at first reflected upon all the ways in which those who already believed after baptism were assisted by the Spirit. Thus we read in Acts 5:32 that God has given the Holy Spirit to those who obey him. That is not something that happens merely on a single occasion. Although the Spirit conditions the whole of a person's life (Acts 2:38; 9:17; 19:2), yet on specific occasions he is given anew. This is what happens to Peter when he is brought before the Sanhedrin in defense of his faith (4:8), or to the whole church after this episode (4:31). It also happens to Paul when he is attacked by a pagan magician (13:9), and to Stephen—who even before his election was "full of the Spirit and wisdom" (6:3)—in his dispute with the Sanhedrin. The community thus learned by experience that the Holy Spirit is a lifelong gift, although never a possession over which it had command and control. Especially at times of trouble and fear did it experience a fresh outpouring of the gift of the Spirit. That is why, in Luke particularly, the community relied so much on prayer. Luke alone of all the evangelists mentions that Jesus himself prayed before the Holy Spirit descended upon him (Luke 3:21). Similarly in Acts 8:15 and 9:9–11 the community prays before it receives the Spirit for the first time, and in 4:31 and 13:1–3 when it receives the Spirit again, while according to Luke 11:13 the Father gives the Spirit from heaven only to those who ask for it.

The Spirit as Encouragement and Guidance in Preaching the Gospel

The community then, experienced the Spirit in the courage through which it was able to preach Jesus in a hostile world. This is what their Lord had promised them in Acts 1:8. Peter even says that the apostles are witnesses of Jesus *and* the Holy Spirit (Acts 5:32). Likewise we are told that Apollos was fervent in spirit when he preached Jesus (18:25). The community experienced the help of the Spirit not only in courts of law but also where it surrendered to his guidance in its preaching and tried to listen to God before taking off on its own. Thus the Spirit showed the church how to proceed in proclaiming the gospel and how not to. Philip was sent to the Ethiopian treasurer (8:29); Peter, against his own wishes, to the Gentile Cornelius (10:19; 11:12); Paul and Barnabas on their first missionary journey (13:2, 4). It is important for Luke that it was to the Gentiles that the Spirit led them. Right at the outset, in his inaugural sermon (which is peculiar to Luke) Jesus, with "the Spirit of the Lord upon him" (Luke 4:18), reminds his hearers that long ago Elijah and Elisha were sent to Gentiles while Israel refused to listen (vv. 24–27). And whether it was a physical illness, which Paul accepted as a sign from the Holy Spirit (Acts 16:6–7; probably to be interpreted in the light of Gal. 4:13), or whether it was a dream (16:9) that stopped him, Paul is prevented by the Spirit from doing missionary work where he really wanted to.

In fact there is still more to be said. Since Luke connects the Spirit so closely with Jesus (see p. 54), it makes no difference for him whether it is "the Holy Spirit" (Acts 16:6), "the Spirit of Jesus" (16:7), "God" (16:10), or "the Lord Jesus" (18:9) who directs the course of Paul's missionary journeys. In a certain sense God, the risen Jesus Christ, and the Holy Spirit are one and the same. God shows us his "heart" or his "face" only in Jesus, and in the Spirit this becomes present to us. Hence the Spirit can speak in personal terms: "*I* have sent them" (10:20), or "Set apart for me Barnabas and Saul" (13:2; cf. 16:6; 21:11).[7] In the Spirit God speaks to us in person. Yet it is not a matter of complete indifference whether Luke speaks of the Spirit of God or of Christ. If he speaks of Christ he is trying to emphasize the authority of the directive—God and the risen Christ are speaking from heaven. If he speaks of the Spirit, he is emphasizing God's work in man—the Spirit penetrates the heart. Of course these ways of speaking cannot be completely separated. But Luke and probably the community in which he lived had not learned to ascribe their faith to the work of the Spirit. "Faith" surely arose "through him," that is, through the Lord Jesus Christ. Indeed, it was the Lord who opened people's hearts (3:16; 16:14). But here Luke is thinking more of Christ as he approaches a person in the preaching and calls him to turn and repent (2:38; 3:19). The Spirit on the other hand is the power which enables the believers to become preachers of Jesus Christ. Again, the power of the Spirit to penetrate the thoughts of others and resist their attack successfully is helpful in their preaching. Thus Paul discerns in the Holy Spirit the intentions of the pagan sorcerer and strikes him blind (13:9). The same sort of thing happens with Peter and those two members of the community, Ananias and Sapphira, who "lied to the Holy Spirit" and were punished by death (5:3, 9), and with the prophets who can tell the future (11:28; 20:23; 21:4, 11).[8]

The beginnings of the Pauline mission to the Gentiles are marked by a tremendous thrust forward, whereas the time after the apostle's death could be better described as a time of holding fast to the faith. As early as Acts 9:31, preaching the gospel to the community in "normal" peaceful times is understood as "comfort of the Holy Spirit." In Paul's farewell speech at Miletus, which looks foward to the time after his death, the leaders of the community are told that the Holy Spirit had appointed "guardians" (the same term as "bishop") to feed the flock (20:28). This contemplates the prospect of persecution and false teaching. As for Paul himself, in the final stage of his life the

Spirit foretells persecution for him and at the same time "binds" him not to avoid it, but to bear witness as a martyr to his faith (20:22–23). The two things of course go together: there is no other way of missionary preaching than for the preacher himself to live by the gospel, even if it means tribulation and persecution. But there are times when the spread of the gospel has priority, and other times when its preservation comes first. Luke is convinced that a community which does not preach Jesus, which does not radiate contagious power, has ceased to belong to Jesus. In fact, so firmly is Luke convinced of this that he really speaks of the Spirit only in this connection.

There may also be a deeper reason for this. The Holy Spirit manifests to us above all the living and present God as One whom we can never "hire" once and for all and adopt for our own possession. That is why Luke tells us how God in his Spirit is constantly intervening in the life of the community, issuing new orders. God remains the One who is constantly en route toward new people and new shores. He cannot be detained at the place where he happens to be at the moment. We cannot as it were observe him from the outside and think we now know once and for all just what the Holy Spirit is. The community's experience of the Spirit was such that he continued to lead it and direct it toward those who were in special need of the gospel. So convinced were they that God was alive, so strong was the missionary emphasis in the early church, that they gave little thought to the broader work of the Spirit in the whole range of daily life, in the keeping of the commandments, and in making the right decisions in many practical questions. That is something we shall find in Paul.

THE HOLY SPIRIT AS THE
REVEALER OF THE
CRUCIFIED: PAUL

The Strength of the Weak

Paul reflected more deeply than anyone else on the work of the Holy Spirit. But he is not all that easy to understand, and so we must take particular care in following his train of thought. He too emphasizes that he had preached Christ "in demonstration of the Spirit and power" (1 Cor. 2:4; cf. p. 64). Without doubt the Spirit is for him as for others a help in preaching. But how strange that the object of his preaching is Jesus Christ the Crucified. And in this connection Paul insists that he does not wish to know of anything else (v. 2). His Lord is thus the One who "was crucified in weakness, but lives by the power of God." And the Lord's messengers are imbued by the same power in weakness: they too "are weak in him but shall live with him in the power of God" (2 Cor. 13:4). Therefore for Paul the saying is true, "when I am weak, then I am strong" (2 Cor. 12:10). The "demonstration of the Spirit and power" is therefore not a simple thing to pinpoint. It is in the crucified Jesus that we find God's reality most clearly. This is "what no eye has seen, nor ear heard, nor the heart of man conceived," and what God has revealed to us through the Spirit. It is for this purpose that "we have received . . . the Spirit which is from God, that we might understand the gifts bestowed on us by God." Human wisdom can certainly not understand this, only he who is laid hold of by the Spirit. Thus the crucified Jesus is certainly "the wisdom of God," but for him who knows nothing of the Spirit he is sheer "folly" (1 Cor. 1:18–2:16). This then is the decisive work of the Spirit, that a man can no longer escape from Jesus, from the One who on the cross is able to let go of everything except his Father in heaven, so that in him the will of man and the will of God become one.

The Spirit of Faith

That God in his Spirit enters our world like a stranger is not merely shown in various miracles performed by Jesus or his disciples. Of course the community is deeply grateful for that. But such things are not basically different from what other great men and women can do. It is still too much like what man can achieve when he is at the height of success. The unheard-of thing, the thing completely alien to man, is something entirely different. God travels in the other direction: He is God in the very act of descending to the deepest depths in Jesus. And Jesus does not rebel against his destiny or throw in the sponge. He does not even hide his disappointment or suppress his resistance until in the end he explodes. God is God, a God who is strange to us because he can do what we cannot – succumb to weakness and powerlessness for our sake. The Holy Spirit, then, is the One who binds us to Jesus, not first and foremost by giving us impressive gifts of the Spirit like healing, prophecy, and a fervent faith, not by enabling us to distinguish Jesus from all others as the One begotten by the Spirit, but first and foremost by teaching us to be weak with him and to experience in that weakness the power of God. This is what Paul means by justification. God's power begins where we experience his judgment over us, and our eyes are opened to what is both right *and* wrong with ourselves. For then we know that it does not matter how we see ourselves or how others see us, warts and all; what matters is God's intention toward us. That is why Paul can speak of the "spirit of faith" (2 Cor. 4:13), and the "Spirit as a guarantee" in which we "walk by faith," which is not yet the "sight" of the glory of God (5:5, 7).

SPIRIT AND FLESH: PAUL
Two Powers?

Paul made a most perceptive attempt to pin down the difference between "spirit" and "flesh," a difference we find hard to grasp. This distinction had harmful consequences because it was very soon understood in a sense different from that which Paul had in mind. Under the influence of current Greek thought and the Platonic tradition (see p. 29) "flesh" was equated for centuries with the physical side of human nature and especially with human sexuality. The "spirit" on the other hand was more or less equated with human thought, our higher feelings, and our ideals. This is how Galatians 5:17 was interpreted when it says "the flesh lusteth against the spirit, and the spirit against the flesh for these are contrary the one to the other; that ye may not do the things that ye would" [RV, with "spirit" in lower case].

Does this not look like a picture of an idealistic person who really wants to be good, but constantly succumbs, for example, to his sexual desires? Such a notion reminds us of the Jewish ascetics at Qumran who spoke of the two spirits fighting for man (see p. 34), or of Philo, who learned from Plato that the passions of the body are the offspring of the flesh, bringing enslavement and suffering for the soul, which comes from heaven (see p. 39). Now Paul himself was probably affected by that sort of thinking too. Influence from that quarter is suggested by Paul's constant use of the terms *flesh* and *spirit,* and also by the way he divides people into two groups, one group living according to the flesh, and the other according to the Spirit. But the real question is whether he means the same thing as did the people of Qumran or Philo. Paul had just been reminding the Galatians (Gal. 3:2–5) that they had begun their life as Christians in "the Spirit," "by hearing with faith," and so they cannot go on living "in the flesh," that is, "by the works of the law." Similarly in the Epistle to the Romans "the new life of the Spirit" is contrasted with "the old life of the flesh," that is, the life under the law which leads us into sin. Or again Paul contrasts the "Spirit" and the "letter," that is, the written law (7:5–6; 2:29). The "flesh" is alive at the very point where a person wants to be obedient to the law of God. But as in the Old Testament, so too in Paul, the opposite to "flesh" is usually not the "Spirit" but God himself. The "wise according to the flesh" are contrasted with "the wisdom of God" (1 Cor. 1:26), the "fleshly wisdom" [RSV earthly] with the "grace of God" (2 Cor. 1:12), "fleshly" [RSV worldly] weapons with that which "has divine power" (10:4), boasting "according to the flesh" [RSV of worldly things] with speaking "with the Lord's authority" (11:17–18), while "the children of the flesh" are contrasted to "the children of promise" (Rom. 9:8). The sharpest contrast is found in Philippians 3:3–7: Paul had "confidence in the flesh" prior to his calling by Christ, that is, he trusted in his membership in the people of God and in his "blamelessness" under the law. But now he regards all that as "refuse" and puts his whole confidence in Jesus Christ, who has become his "boast." That is the service of God "in the Spirit." So the question is, what does a man build his life on? "Flesh," as in the Old Testament, is everything human and earthly, man's thoughts and even his moral endeavors, no less than his money or his sexuality. Whether his concerns are principally physical, psychological, or cerebral makes no difference: man is more concerned with the earthly and human than he is with God.

This is demonstrated by a peculiar turn of speech. The "spiritual" man is contrasted not only with the "fleshly," but even more emphatically with the "psychical." Even before Paul, Philo had connected the soul of man with the "earth," which God cursed after the Fall (*Allegorical Interpretation* 3. 247). It is from this earth that the soul stems, with all those impulses that are opposed to God. This idea was obviously widespread at the time. For in the New Testament the Epistle of James contrasts the "unspiritual wisdom" [lit. psychical] which is "earthly and devilish" with the "wisdom from above" (James 3:15). Likewise the Epistle of Jude calls the ungodly man, who lives only for his appetites, "psychical" [RSV worldly] (Jude 19). In similar terms Paul speaks in 1 Corinthians 2:14; 15:44–49 of the "spiritual" and "psychical" [RSV unspiritual] (see p. 113). Such a person is for Paul not demonic, but simply man in his earthly nature with his earthly soul, whose options are still open and who can still choose whether he wants to turn to God or to the "flesh."

The "Moral" Flesh

It is necessary, however, to go a step further. The moralist, who knows so exactly what is good and what is evil, is the one who has the deepest roots in the "flesh." The adulterer and the murderer generally know there is much that is wrong with them. They really have great need for God, even if they deny his existence. The moralist by contrast does not notice it. He thinks he has God in his pocket. He looks down his nose at everyone else, laying down the law, pitying them or getting annoyed because their lives are so much more immoral than his. As a matter of fact, by behaving in that way he is placing more confidence in the "flesh," in nothing but the "flesh," in the very successes he has achieved by dint of vigorous self-discipline. This is what makes him unbearable. You can imagine what absolute hell life with a perfect wife or a perfect husband must be! The perfect person is a standing reproach to others. We can't expect him to help us for if we come before him we can do so only as the very people he rightly accuses of every sin in the book. So according to Paul it is the pious, law-abiding moralist who is "in the flesh," he who is "blameless" as regards the righteousness demanded by the law.

What is true for all mankind became evident in Israel in a unique way. Man lives far from God. This is true not only of our hours of weakness, not only when life is at a low ebb, when we behave like beasts, relinquishing our self-control and yielding to all our desires; it is just as true where we are devout and righteous and take ourselves more seriously than we take God. Even where we are not out for power, wealth, or pleasure but — being the moralists we are — simply revolve around ourselves, full of inferiority complexes or of the conviction that we "have made it at long last," we are still concerned only with ourselves. We still rely on the flesh instead of throwing ourselves entirely on the love of God and living on that love. That is why Paul can say that it was the law, oddly enough, that brought sin to its peak (Rom. 5:20), to the point where sin could hide behind a perfection unquestionable from a moralistic point of view, so that no one would notice how unloving and self-centered sin is. And it is just here, according to Paul, that the tables are turned. Only the person who realizes that all his moralistic efforts have failed to make him one whit more lovable or brought him any closer to God, is truly receptive for God and his gracious advent. Before that a man could only dream of making it some day in the future and becoming more perfect. But now he knows that only God can rescue him from his alienation. Now at last he no longer has to revolve around himself and ask himself how good or wicked he is.

Of course it is shocking to have to say all this. God loves us no less if we come to him with dirty hands than if we have achieved perfection in the sight of the law. Man does not have to earn God's love; indeed, man is unable to do so. If by any chance man does do God's will and lets God use him (see pp. 87–88), he does so entirely for God's sake, without so much as a glance at his own perfection or imperfection. There is now no need for a person to be so worried about keeping his hands clean. He can take the risk of failure. There is no need to retire to some hiding place where a minimum of responsibility awaits him, where there is little risk of making a mistake. Luther saw this when he wrote to a hesitant, overscrupulous correspondent: "Sin boldly!" In the Gospel of Mark the first man to recognize Jesus as the Son of God was not a cleric, soiled as little as possible by the world and its injustices, but an officer of the occupying power, a man who had participated in the crucifixion of Jesus, cruelly executing an innocent man, an executioner who might one day be punished as a war criminal for what he had done (Mark 15:39).

The Spirit as the Almighty
Power of God

By "flesh" Paul means all human behavior, or more precisely all human life which looks for salvation to its own frantic efforts. By "Spirit" Paul means the action of God himself, which man experiences as a gift that comes upon him and makes him happy, sets him free and makes his life responsible and meaningful. This can be shown by a further observation. In Galatians 4:23 Paul tells of the two children of Abraham. The first was begotten "according to the flesh," when Abraham was confident in earthly and human possibilities. Since Sarah was too old, Abraham took a young servant maid as his mistress and she bore him a son. But after that Sarah bore him another son through a divine miracle. Paul calls this second son "the child of promise." In Philippians 3:3 Paul contrasts the worship of God "in spirit" with confidence "in the flesh," and in Romans 8:13–14 the "life according to the flesh" with "life through [RSV by] the Spirit." Here "flesh" is what man looks to and trusts. On the other hand "Spirit" is God himself at work granting us life and service. Strictly speaking, Spirit is the only power that can achieve anything, for it is the power of God himself. The "flesh" is simply what lies at hand. It is everything that is earthly and human. This means that flesh is not in and of itself evil, for it is God's creation. It only becomes evil in its effects if we set all our hope upon it and forget about God. Of course it can become a power, but only when we confer power upon it. It is like alcohol, which can become an evil "power" if a man surrenders to it and becomes addicted, though alcohol in and of itself is not evil and can be beneficially used, to cleanse wounds, for example. Likewise everything earthly and human, even our attempts to become as righteous as we can, may become an evil power and make us its victims. This happens, not because such striving is in itself that kind of evil power, but because without God man gives it so much power over himself. By contrast, the Spirit of

God is the real power, for the Spirit is God himself at work within us.

In Galatians 5 the difference emerges very clearly. Here Paul speaks of the *"works* of the flesh" which are plain, but of the *"fruit* of the Spirit" (Gal. 5:19). Works are the things we do, the things we achieve on our own, whereas fruit grows by itself. On the one hand there is the attitude which expects our own works to give us everything, whether we are piling up our assets, going from one sexual affair to another, rising from one position of power to another, and in the process ruining ourselves and our fellow men with our money, sex, or lust for power, or achieving the same result with our moralism. The alternative to such perpetual striving is the life in which we let God do his work. That is why Paul puts "works" in the plural but "fruit" in the singular. That's just the point; you can pile up your "works" and count them. Every evening you can look back over the day that is past and, depending on your temperament, write it all off as garbage, or bask in your success. But "fruit" has a wholeness about it. It describes a life that for all its light and shadow, its good deeds and mistakes, is directed toward God, knowing even that God can sometimes use our failures better than our successes. Of course Peter would not have been Peter if he had not been able to devote himself to Jesus as his Lord, even to the point of death. But Peter has been a source of blessing for centuries because we can read so much about his cowardice both before Easter (Mark 14:66–72) and after (Gal. 2:11–14). Millions of people have learned from him to live happy and comfortable with their God — despite all their imperfections.

THE HOLY SPIRIT IN THE LIFE OF
THE COMMUNITY: PAUL

Thus the Spirit embraces life as a whole. It is not just a knowledge of God affecting only our minds. What happens according to Paul when a person receives a gift of the Spirit?

Freedom

The answer at first sight is extremely simple. The Spirit, Paul tells us, reveals Jesus as the crucified One. That means, there is no escaping this man Jesus, who after a very short period of public ministry went deliberately, but with no particular heroism, to the cross. There is no escaping until we realize that this was a life that liberates, giving meaning to our own lives. Of course we are really free only when we acknowledge that Jesus is not just a model to be copied, not just a pioneer for us to follow, but an offer from God which we can only accept as a gift. If it is true that Jesus shows us by the way he lived and died who God really is, then the power of God really exists in weakness. Then it is equally true of us that God accepts us for Jesus Christ's sake, in all our weakness and not only when we are on top of things. There is no longer any need for man to pay attention to his "flesh," his external fortunes, his innate talents or his failures. This is what Paul means by "justification." This is so important to Paul that the only thing he can compare with the entering of the Spirit into man's life is the freeing of a slave from all his fear (Rom. 8:15–16, 21; Gal. 4:6–7, 25–26; 5:1–5). "Now where the Spirit of the Lord is, there is freedom" (2 Cor. 3:17), almost incredible freedom. No law hems us in any longer, not even the law of self-perfection. God loves us before we achieve anything at all. "In this is love, not that we loved God but that he loved us" (1 John 4:10), or in Paul's own words: "God shows his love for us in that while we were yet sinners Christ died for us" (Rom. 5:8). Because of this we need no longer live in constant fear of appearing inadequate in our own eyes or in the eyes of our fellow men. There is no need to go on searching frantically for our own identity — it has been given to us from the outset.

Prayer

Hence for Paul the characteristic gift of the Spirit is the ability to pray. We learn to say, "Abba, Father" (Gal. 4:6–7; Rom. 8:15–17). We know that God is not just some distant or mysterious power, to be feared or ignored because we know nothing definite about him. No, God seeks to share our life because he loves us so much. So his first and foremost gift is not a power enabling us to do greater things, but the gift of prayer. In prayer we can let God do as he pleases, even if we are sometimes weak and looking elsewhere for strength. This is of such stupendous importance to Paul that he can even say that we do not know how to pray aright, and that the Spirit has to translate our foolish prayers before God can hear them aright (Rom. 8:26–27; see p. 110). Not even prayer is our own achievement. It is like a child being allowed to speak to his mother after they have had a row; the child doesn't think of doing anything to deserve it. Jesus himself knew this when he said we need not use many words as though we were trying to earn God's help by the length of our prayers. God knows already what we need, even before we open our mouths. It is not a duty but a privilege to say: "Our Father who art in heaven . . ." (Matt. 6:7–13).

Sanctification

But this privilege does not come by accident. If anyone learns to use the gift of the Spirit as a basis for his life, it leaves its mark on him. You might say: he is now living in a different "atmosphere," which encompasses him and penetrates all his pores, as in the case of a person suffering from tuberculosis who is removed to a higher altitude to recover his health. So Paul says in the same section of Romans (8:1–10) that we now live "in Christ" or in "the Spirit" and so "Christ" or the "Spirit" is also living "in us." Thus the Spirit, that power which we receive as a sheer gift from God, becomes the norm of our lives. We learn, when faced with a dilemma, to distinguish between right and wrong, and Paul sees that too as a gift of the Spirit (1 Cor. 7:40). This is no new law. The Spirit never leads us to—in Paul's words—"put a rope around each others' necks." But we are making enough progress to stop worrying about the "flesh" and to look for what the Spirit has to offer us. There we find true life and peace. For here what God requires of us "is fulfilled in us," not just through us but within us, for the best in our lives comes to us as a gift. The more relaxed we are and the more naturally we live, without too much navel-gazing, the better it will be (Rom. 8:4–6). In Galatians 6:8 Paul uses a different figure of speech to make the same point. What matters most is where a man sows, and where he expects the corresponding fruit to come from: the "flesh" that is his own or the "Spirit" that is not his.

For this reason washing, sanctification, and justification are all one and the same gift of the Spirit (1 Cor. 6:11). In Jesus "our sins are washed away." All our disappointments and failures are covered up because God accepts us as we are. Through him we are "justified," which means God accepts us, warts and all. But then we are also "sanctified." This means that God takes us to his side where he himself can heal us and use us for the healing of others. This also means that faith is never something that happens once and for all, a decision to accept certain truths, but a whole life with its steady or erratic progress, with all its magnificent achievements or miserable failures. Paul can even say in a discussion of sexual problems that our body has become "the temple of the Holy Spirit." For God himself has "bought us with a price" (1 Cor. 6:20–21). And in a discussion of religious controversies Paul can also make the same point about the community at large, for which God in Christ laid the "foundation" (1 Cor. 3:11, 16). Such is the realism with which Paul contemplates what has happened. If we really are so incredibly important to God, the Lord of the whole universe, that in Jesus he came and sought us out, how could we then be so careless with our bodies and their sexuality, which God wants to use. How could we simply cast them on the refuse heap, or attach such importance to our special religious insights and talents as to let them break up the community? So the Spirit is always the One who "sanctifies" (Rom. 15:16). When we believe like that, the Spirit comes to us again and again as a promise pointing to the future (Gal. 3:14), and we have good hope that we shall be in the right with God, though this can be fulfilled completely only in his own good time (5:5).

Being Open to Others

Above all, the gift of the Spirit makes us open to other human beings. For whoever has been liberated from self is also liberated for the one who needs his love. The person who has no need to amass greedily everything he can lay his hands on acquires free space for others. Thus the tax collector Zacchaeus was freed from his riches for the sake of those who needed his money more urgently than he did (Luke 19:1–10). Thus Paul was liberated from his own righteousness for brotherhood with those who were not as perfect by moralistic standards as he was himself (Phil. 3:6–7). And the same thing happened to Peter for the comfort of millions of people who have read the Gospels (p. 85). So instead of saying that we are now living "in the Spirit" or "in Christ" Paul can say we are living in "the body of Christ." He explicitly associates this in 1 Corinthians 12:13 with the work of the Spirit: "In [RSV by] one Spirit we were all baptized into one body . . . and were all made to drink of one Spirit." The word "body" underscores our solidarity in a living fellowship with all other believers, that is, in the church. Therefore love ("the love of the Spirit," Rom. 15:30) is the first fruit (Gal. 5:22), and in the Hymn to Charity love is called the greatest gift of the Spirit (1 Cor. 12:31–14:1). It is the one gift which includes all others (chap. 12) and so builds up the community (chap. 14; cf. also Romans 12:9a, coming as it does between vv. 3–8 and vv. 9b–13).

THE MANIFOLD VARIETY OF THE GIFTS OF THE SPIRIT: PAUL

The Confession as a Criterion

Here Paul set the signals right for millenia to come because all his life long he never abandoned the crucified One but probed to the depths what this Jesus meant for himself and for the community. Paul does not deny that there are healings, prophecies, and speaking in tongues which are the gifts of the Spirit. But he reminds the community that it had similar experiences even in its pagan days (1 Cor. 12:2). Paul was fully aware that the peculiarity or strangeness of such experiences is no proof that the Holy Spirit is at work. This depends as before on our temperament, upbringing, and even the climate in which we were raised.

In my small country of Switzerland there are the dour people of Zurich who hardly ever talk about their faith unless they happen to be clergymen, and there are the more relaxed people of Geneva who even find it natural occasionally to end a dance with a prayer. Such things are even more common further south: people from Ticino laugh and cry more readily than northerners and feel everything, even God, with double intensity. God can use both types just as much as the devil can. Sometimes God needs the enthusiasm of the southern Swiss to break through the tedium of his church; at other times he uses the dourness of the northern Swiss to curb what threatens to grow into fanaticism and bring people back on the right road.

Much the same sort of thing could be said of modern charismatic movements. How desperately we need those who experience their faith in "high tension" and can stir into movement what seems to have ground to a halt. But the reverse is equally true. You cannot live your whole life in high tension. The danger then, when the Spirit does not seem to blow with pristine vigor, is that you will start helping things along a little and end up by falling into unconscious pretense because by that time you think you have learned well how the Spirit expresses himself. Experiences which once were startlingly new come to be more or less automatic simply because they are assumed to be integral. This is why the charismatics have need of others who, though open to new movements, know at the same time how the life of all church members, even those who are less "turned on," can go on bearing fruit for decades to come, after the excitement has died down. Paul recognized that the only criterion to distinguish the Holy Spirit from any other kind of enthusiasm lies in the confession: "Jesus is Lord" (1 Cor. 12:3). Of course Paul does not mean that all we need to do is go on repeating these three words. For the creed must be in our hearts no less than on our lips (and the heart, for the Old Testament, includes man's moral will). This is the pitch Paul makes in Romans 10:10. Where the Spirit is at work, whether in remarkable ways or quite ordinary ways, he always exalts Jesus as our Master. If the speaker in tongues seeks the limelight for himself and wants to show off his gift all the time, he becomes the Lord instead of Jesus.

The Love of Neighbor as a Criterion:
Speaking in Tongues and Prophecy

Paul looks at the same thing from the opposite point of view when he emphasizes that the Spirit was given for the use of all (1

Cor. 12:7). For where Jesus is Lord the gifts begin to serve others instead of enhancing the glory of those who possess them. We could also put it like this: Where the Spirit ceases to create and foster community, it is no longer the Spirit of God. Anyone who thinks he has the Spirit, and takes center stage with his gift, who cannot get along with others but founds a party of his own, is no longer the bearer of the Spirit but a "man of flesh"—even when he appeals to Paul's letters themselves (1 Cor. 3:1–4).

This is the problem Paul is dealing with in Corinthians 14. The Corinthians thought those speaking in tongues (see p. 138, note 6) had the greatest gift because it appeared so inexplicable and miraculous. We can easily understand that. We all like to think it is more important, and in fact a greater gift, to be able to pray aloud in public than to pray quietly by ourselves; still more do we admire those who not only say the Lord's Prayer but extemporize and top it off with Bible verses or unusual phrases like those in the liturgy. If that is so, the highest gift of all would certainly be the speaking in tongues. Now Paul has a high regard for speaking in tongues: "I thank God that I speak in tongues more than you all" (1 Cor. 14:18). We have often felt that words were inadequate to express our feelings. For example, we would like to say exactly what we feel about the beauty of the mountains we have gazed at in silence, but we realize how utterly inadequate words can be. All we can do is to cry out for joy. Or perhaps in our love life we may try to express in words what we feel in our hearts, but soon that too becomes inadequate and only the sighs and moans of rapture betray our emotion. How could it be otherwise in prayer when we are so filled with the Spirit that words no longer suffice? Paul however continues: "Nevertheless, in church I would rather speak five words with my mind . . . than ten thousand words in a tongue"— that because he is concerned with the "building up" of the church. The question therefore is whether the Spirit can serve others and build them up. Paul even goes so far as to say that the real test of worship comes when an unbeliever or an uncommitted person drops in. Can the unbeliever understand what we are preaching about? Does it strike home where he actually is? That is the real question (14:23–25). If he cannot say "Amen" to it something has gone wrong (14:16). Whether the hearer assents to the message or not depends, of course, on God, but the hearer must have the option to say Yes or No. It must not come to this, that not having understood a word, he just shrugs his shoulders and leaves without so much as a protest, let alone without being changed by what he has heard.

It is quite possible, even without the gift of tongues, to speak in a tongue, that is, in a language unintelligible to the outsider. The listener may then mumble an Amen at the appropriate places in the liturgy without having understood a single word. Nothing can be worse than that. Where speaking in tongues is genuine, the listener, though he may not understand, will sense that here is someone who in the totality of his being is completely involved with God. But where the hearer is addressed in an alien language, a language which is so technical and theological or popular and meaningless that it does not contain enough love to search out the person where he really is, then the Spirit is simply not present.

In Romans there is another list of charismata, again followed by a reference to outsiders who are not involved with the church and in fact make the church's life difficult. The church has a responsibility for them too (Rom. 12:14, 17–20). But here (apart from v. 11) Paul makes no direct reference to the Spirit. In 1 Corinthians 14 on the other hand he explicitly lays down the rule that those who have the Spirit should not speak all at once but take turns, only two or three at a time (1 Cor. 14:27–29). Of course tremendous excitement is generated when dozens of prophets and speakers in tongues are all competing together. But that is not the life of the Holy Spirit, for the Spirit is concerned to build up the church. He does not go on chattering—he sees those who come empty and hungering and who ought to hear the right word. That is why "the spirits of the prophets are subject to the prophets" (KJV 14:32), and should be judged by the community.

Of course this is all very shocking. It soon comes to be accepted in the church that under no circumstances should anyone speaking in tongues be criticized. That would be a sin against the Holy Ghost (*Didache* 11:7). The Spirit speaks only when the human will is eliminated (Hermes, *Man.* 9:8). Under coercion of the Spirit a person can hold forth for two hours without being able to stop (*Mart. Pol.* 7:2). That is what the Greeks, influenced by Plato, thought, and this is how Philo pictured it (see pp. 00–00). But Paul realizes that the all-embracing gift of the Spirit is love: "If I speak in the tongues of men and angels, but have not love, I am a noisy gong or a clanging cymbal" (1 Cor. 13:1). It is only love that matters, not the psychology of speaking in the Spirit.

WHAT DOES THIS MEAN?

Paul sees the Spirit really at work when the crucified Jesus encounters a human being and will not let him go. Such an encounter has the remarkable effect of turning all our standards of strength and weakness upside down. The most spectacular religious achievement may be nothing, and a completely insignificant act not seen by anyone but God may turn out to be the work of the Holy Spirit. That is why Paul puts speaking in tongues in 1 Corinthians 12:10 and 28 at the very bottom of the list. It is not because it is not a sign of an intensive spiritual life but because it can do little to help other people.[9]

And for the same reason there is no hierarchy of gifts. In Romans 12:7 the deacon comes before the teacher—before his theological professor! In 1 Corinthians 12:28 the deacon comes immediately after the apostle and prophet. Sometimes one gift is regarded as the greatest or most important and sometimes another, depending on which one God needs at any given time. It is interesting to compare the two lists in 1 Corinthians 12:28 and 29–30: they are identical except that the second one drops the gifts of social service, care, and leadership (or are these gifts concerned with organization?)—probably because no one really wanted them. In verses 29–30 Paul asks: "Are all apostles? Are all prophets?" The Corinthians did not think there was anything religious about social service or leadership. To prepare a meal for the sick, you don't need the Spirit but a cooking pot, and to sweep a church you need a broom. And to chair a meeting all you need is a little talent for organization. But Paul knows that care of the sick and institutional administration are just as much gifts of the Holy Spirit as speaking in tongues, prophecy, and prayer.

What Paul says sounds unbelievably austere. If out of love for his church a trained bookkeeper straightens out its accounts, the Holy Spirit is just as much at work as if the bookkeeper had given an inspiring sermon, gone out full of enthusiasm as a missionary, prayed with great emotion, or even spoken in tongues. The Corinthians had had overwhelming religious experiences even in their pagan days. In fact it is always a matter of one's "natural" gifts (cf. pp. 89–90). For the Spirit of God is the Spirit of all creation. But it is better to put it the other way round: Every gift is "supernatural." For when God uses a person's gifts it is anything but natural (cf. pp. 59–60). If anyone speaks casually of Jesus there is nothing out of the ordinary about that. But once God uses that person's words to speak to another person and call him to faith the miracle of the Spirit has happened in the fullness of its power. If anyone speaks in tongues or heals the sick through prayer that is something extraordinary but it is not a miracle. It is a gift which is submerged in most people but emerges here and there without the person involved necessarily having anything to do with God. But if God needs this gift to call the person to faith it certainly becomes a miracle of the Holy Spirit, no less but no more than in the first case. Yet there are times when God has to use extraordinary gifts if he is to make himself heard at all, and when that happens we should be very grateful indeed. Then there are other times when the primary need is for ordinary gifts. Both may be very important, depending on the nature of the case. But it does not mean that extraordinary gifts are any more miraculous or supernatural than the ordinary ones. We are not suggesting that speaking in tongues or healing of the sick are purely natural occurrences. The point is that not only those gifts but also social service and intelligible speech are to be recognized as incredible miracles of the Holy Spirit once they are permitted to bring people to faith, give them comfort, or lead them to love.

This is how Paul understands it. He speaks about it in three parallel sentences (1 Cor. 12:4–6). It is a matter of "gifts of grace" granted by the Holy Spirit. This brings out the fact that it is an event which in the last resort is rooted in God's world, and therefore comes "from above." This is particularly emphasized by the reference to "Spirit." Alongside this vertical line there is a horizontal one. The gift of grace is always "service" to the neighbor as the Lord grants it. This is made especially clear in connection with Jesus, for he himself lived a life of service and expected the same of his disciples. And finally, the "working" is the work of God himself. That is why Paul speaks in this context of "God who works all things in all" [following KJV].

Hence the variety of gifts belong together like the members of a body (vv. 14–25). In the church there is no place for inferiority complexes. The ear cannot say that because it is not an eye it does not really belong to the body. We appreciate the point the ear is making, of course. There it is, attached to the side of the head, perhaps completely hidden by the hair so that no one can see it. A young man gazes into the eyes of his girl friend but he would never look into her ears. So an inconspicuous member of the church may similarly think he is no good—no one would miss him. The reverse is equally true, says Paul. There is no place for self-importance in the community. An eye cannot say it has nothing to do with the hands. Here again the eye has a point. It can look down at the world from up above. The hands have to wash up in a filthy bucket. So it is easy to think that things would be much better if we could ignore the dirty and neglected members. But Paul writes: "If the whole body were an eye, where would be the hearing?" Picture a whole body consisting of nothing but a great big eye and a few pieces of skin. At best such a thing would be a terribly deformed birth, fit only to be preserved in alcohol and used to scare medical students. But, says Paul, this is what a church is like when there is only one kind of ministry which has to do everything, for example, when all Christians are clergy. Such a miscegenation would be the fault of both parties, those who in their modesty think they have nothing at all to contribute, and those who are so convinced of their own importance that they are ready to uncouple the slow coaches, the less committed or less gifted members of the community. "If one member suffers, all suffer together" (v. 26). In context this means not only that the church should share the suffering or sickness of the individual member, but that the whole community suffers if a single member is unable to exercise the service given to him by the Spirit. And "if one member is honored, all rejoice together," even if it is only the least conspicuous, most ordinary gift that is being displayed.

As Paul sees it, the Spirit is at work where Jesus leads a person to the cross and will not let him go (this is what we saw in the first section about Paul). This means an incredible freedom, the freedom of all flesh from those things which ensnare us, including everything from money to religious perfectionism (this became clear in the second section). It frees man from himself (as the third section shows); it frees him to love others and places him in a community with his fellow men. And this freedom is such a serious affair that it enables him to live as a member of the whole body. Perhaps the most crude and surprising manifestation of this freedom occurs when a person no longer needs to shine in his religious life, when he no longer has the urge to attract attention. He can now rejoice in his neighbor's gift as much as in his own. He has no need to show off his piety to others, or to himself, or to God unless it may help someone else, particularly an outsider (this was the main thrust of the fourth section). When a person begins to live like this, it is because the Spirit has given the crucified Jesus to him in such a way that part of this crucified Lord has entered his heart.

THE HOLY SPIRIT AS
REVEALER OF THE
CRUCIFIED: JOHN

If we examine the Gospel of John under the same headings and in the same sequence as we did the Pauline Epistles, both the agreements and the differences between John and Paul will be laid bare. Many insights, first worked out by Paul half a century earlier, have by the time of John come to be generally accepted. But John often underscores quite different aspects of the Spirit's work from those that Paul had emphasized in his day.

We have mentioned the dialogue between Jesus and Nicodemus about being born again (pp. 70–72). Here we must insist that, like Paul, John is concerned with the message of the crucified Son of man (John 3:14–15). But unlike Paul, John does not emphasize the weakness of the Crucified One, nor the strange law of God whereby God's power is particularly at work in weakness. On the contrary, the cross is the "lifting up" of the Son of man. True, it is a very strange kind of lifting up, a lifting up to the cross. John never dwells on the pain, the dereliction, or the terror of the cross. Even in 12:27 where Jesus says, "Now is my soul troubled," a correction is immediately introduced: he sees in this only God's way. When Jesus says "I thirst," it is only to fulfill the Scripture, not because he is really thirsty (19:28). John has dropped all reference to Jesus' dying cry, neither does John report that word from the cross: "My God, my God, why hast thou forsaken me?" (Mark 15:34, 37). He gives only the triumphant cry: "It is accomplished" (NEB John 19:30). Again, in the dialogue with Nicodemus, the Crucified is the One to whom all must look for life and healing. In fact, John explicitly emphasizes that the Son of man descended from heaven, and has ascended thither again (3:13). He is, as John says immediately afterwards, in deed and truth the judge. Where the Spirit can fashion a man anew so completely that he learns to live with Jesus, such a man has found life indeed; he has already passed through judgment. But where that fails to happen, he has been judged already (v. 18). The same point is made even more clearly in 5:24, where the term *word* is used instead of *Spirit:* "Truly, truly, I say to you, he who hears my word and believes him who sent me, has eternal life; he does not come into judgment, but has passed from death to life." Encounter with Jesus is of such tremendous importance to the fourth evangelist that it embraces much more than merely the past and our emancipation from everything for which we may be judged, much more than merely the present in which the only life worthy of the name is that which in Jesus has found its meaning and achieved its goal; it embraces the future as well in which life like this will abide for ever (see pp. 115–17).

But again, according to John 11:49–52, the Spirit is the Revealer of the Crucified One. That is why the high priest votes for the execution of Jesus out of purely political considerations. It is better for one to die for the people than for all to be brought to ruin, which is what would happen if Jesus caused a popular uprising and the Romans had to intervene. But this, says John, he "prophesied" in his capacity as high priest that year. For Jesus did in fact die for the whole people, though in a very different sense, and beyond that for those who were scattered abroad. So John does not speak here of the weakness and despair of Jesus at his death, but of its meaning of victory which the Spirit discloses to the believer. This is indeed a remarkable claim.

John's understanding of the Spirit's prophesying is similar to Philo's conception of inspiration (pp. 31–32). At the same time it contains an echo of the experiences of early Israel (pp.10–11). The Spirit comes upon us as a stranger. He can speak even where we have not a clue as to his real meaning. Be it noted, however, that John never mentions the speaking in tongues that attracts outside attention. Yet he knows that the word of God can fill an apparently unintelligible human utterance with an entirely different meaning from what the speaker intends. This is something we constantly experience when we engage in deep conversation, even if it does not lead to such an extreme that the new meaning turns out to be almost the exact opposite of the original meaning. It is an experience which makes all preaching, and especially genuine pastoral counseling, possible. It is the experience of the Holy Spirit lending power and penetration to the weak and often stupid word of man.

SPIRIT AND FLESH: JOHN

Heaven and Earth

The strong emphasis on the majesty of Jesus is equally apparent where John contrasts the Spirit with the flesh. He uses the same terms as Paul, but puts the accent elsewhere. In this he is following a long-standing tradition. In pre-Christian Judaism people imagined that spiritual beings, such as angels and perhaps ideal archetypes of the earthly world, lived in heaven, whereas fleshly creatures were condemned to live on earth (see p. 39). The New Testament community therefore interpreted Jesus' resurrection as his entry into the world of the Spirit (see p. 55). This is John's starting point, and at first sight it looks as though he is simply speaking of a "world of the Spirit in heaven above," and of an "evil world of the flesh on earth." This would be similar to contemporary Greek thought, which distinguished between a heavenly, ideal world and a material, imperfect earthly world which only weighs down the soul. "To be born of the Spirit" in John means the same thing as "to be born from above" (John 3:3, 6) or "to be born of God" (1:13; 1 John 3:9). John sees two alternatives: Either one comes "from above," that is, from heaven, or one is "from the earth" (John 3:31). Either one is "from above" and therefore "of God," or one is "from below," which is equivalent to "from this world," "from the devil" (8:23, 42, 44, 47; 15:19; 17:14, 16). Jesus tells Nicodemus he cannot understand "heavenly things" because he is not from above, not born of the Spirit (3:12). Does John mean that the believer should escape from this world as fast as he can and settle in "heaven" with his exalted Lord? Should he in heart and mind, even during his earthly life, dwell only in heaven?

Heaven on Earth

But this cannot be John's meaning. There is not a single passage about the Spirit which describes a life in heaven. The Spirit lives on this earth. What John wants to bring out with all the clarity he can muster is something even the Old Testament prophets knew. In the Spirit God descends in person to man. Man is no longer in dialogue only with himself, probing the deepest depths of his own soul. Rather he is allowed to hear the liberating word coming "from above." Yet this is not just a mysterious event surpassing all other earthly events. In the same passage in which he speaks of "below" and "above," of "this world" and "the other world," of "God" and "the devil," Jesus says: "If you continue in my word, you are truly my disciples, and you will know the truth, and the truth will make you free" (John 8:31–32). Heaven, or the world above, is therefore to be found in Jesus' word. In him heaven has come down to earth. This is that other life, a life which has rediscovered its meaning. It is like life after the creation, when "God saw everything that he had made, and behold, it was very good" (Gen. 1:31). Jesus' words are "spirit and life" (John 6:63). He "utters the words of God, for it is not by measure that he gives the Spirit" (3:34).

99

This has nothing to do with the antithesis between the spiritual and the material. Jesus' familiar saying, "God is spirit, and those who worship him must worship him in spirit and truth" (4:24), does not mean a purely internal worship. To be sure, Jesus does speak against those who claim that only under their auspices can people worship God aright. But this is no retreat into inwardness and subjectivity. Rather it breaks out of all previous limits into the community where even rank outsiders can find a home and all may become one (10:16; 17:21). And this is not just an interior union, but a highly external being-for-one-another. The First Epistle of John says: "If any one has this world's goods and sees his brother in need, yet closes his heart against him, how does God's love abide in him?" (3:17). The same point that was clearly made above comes out here again. The Spirit lives where a person realizes that in Jesus God —and God's new world—comes upon him, sets him straight, and claims him for his own.

Hence we must note that John holds both truths together: In Jesus heaven has come down to earth, the eternal Word has become earthly flesh (John 1:14); just as Jesus wanders about the earth and shares the troubles of his fellow men, so too his disciple must live on this earth and be concerned about not only his own troubles but also those of his fellow men. Yet at the same time Jesus — and his disciple too — lives "from above," in all that he does and suffers being determined by God.

THE HOLY SPIRIT IN THE
LIFE OF THE
COMMUNITY: JOHN

The Spirit of Freedom

Like Paul, John talks about the freedom of the believers, contrasting it with an earlier state of bondage and describing faith as a transition from the status of slavery to that of a son or a child (John 8:32–36). Of course John is speaking in this context of the liberating word of Jesus. But just as this word enables a person to "know the truth" so, after Jesus' resurrection, it is the "Spirit of truth" who will guide his disciples into "all truth" (14:17; 16:13). Yet John's emphasis is different from Paul's. True, John is as concerned as Paul with liberation from "sin." But sin is no longer man's bondage to the law, in a life where his morality and piety constantly revolve around himself. Rather, sin is man's failure to recognize Jesus as the messenger of God, a failure which leads man to nail Jesus to the cross (8:37, 40). This is shown by the frequent use of the word "truth," as something which has to be "known." Thus, unlike Paul, John has nothing to say about all the things a person builds his life upon, things which are mere "flesh," like money, sexuality, or even legalism. John is concerned about one thing only, the truth which the Spirit gives: "This is eternal life, that they know thee, the only true God, and Jesus Christ whom thou has sent" (17:3). In an almost unbelievable concentration everything boils down to a single occurrence—the recognition that in Jesus God himself meets us face to face. In the last analysis Paul says the same thing too. Paul, however, emphasizes that the believer not only gains a new insight, but learns to live it out in thousands of practical, everyday decisions. In these decisions the believer must learn to build no longer upon the flesh but upon what God's Spirit reveals to him as a new way. The apostle seeks to help the process forward with his very practical directions. By contrast, John's experience of the new creation from above was so radical that he sets all his hopes upon the Spirit and upon the truth the Spirit granted him.

Of course, John knows that the believers are living in this world and therefore in community with others, and it is the Spirit which draws them to others: "Out of his heart shall flow rivers of living water (namely, the Spirit)" (John 7:38–39). Again this can only mean the witness about Jesus which the Holy Spirit will give them, and to which they will have to remain faithful, if necessary unto death (15:26–16:2). Just as Jesus' word means freedom from all sin (8:32–36), so the believers' word about Jesus, in which the Holy Spirit is at work, will bring freedom from sins (20:22–23).

The Spirit in the Structure of the Community

The First Epistle of John shows how well the Holy Spirit handles this single task. Unlike Paul, John makes no mention of the various modes of the Spirit's operation. The fact that the members of the community have received the "anointing" of the Holy Spirit (cf. Luke 4:18; 2 Cor. 1:21–22) means that they have all come to "know" and possess the "truth" (1 John 2:20–21). They no longer need anyone to teach them, for what this anointing teaches them is the absolute truth (v. 27). This shows a well-nigh incredible confidence in the power of the Holy Spirit. Just as when Jesus hangs on the cross only his victory is visible, so in the community all we see is the guidance of the Spirit.

This also leaves its mark on John's understanding of the world. Of course he is perfectly aware of the community's responsibility for the world. After all, the world too needs to know that in Jesus the One sent by God has come. Hence the community must proclaim Jesus. But as John sees it, it does this not so much by reaching out beyond its borders as by withdrawing from the world, in order to live deliberately as a community, convincing others with its perfect unity by the power of the indwelling Spirit (John 17:20–23). So there are two different ways of witnessing. One way is to break out of the community as Paul went out into the world, speaking the world's language so that the world can understand the message we would bring about Jesus Christ. We may even go so far as to say that the silent sharing of the world's suffering in everyday, secular life can be the most important missionary service (see p. 130). It is possible, however, to adopt a quite different approach, like John, and lay all our emphasis on the community setting an example to the world by its genuine, relaxed common life under the power of the Spirit. In this respect 1 John can go so far as to say: "Do not love the world or the things in the world . . . the lust of the flesh and the lust of the eyes and the pride of life" (1 John 2:15–16).

Of course John also knows of the love which is Jesus' first commandment. But, for one thing, John mentions only brotherly love, not love of the enemy. And for another, he does not base such love on the work of the Spirit (John 15:12–17; 1 John 3:14–18). Only in 1 John 4:11–13 does he pair the gift of love with the gift of the Spirit, and even there he does not explicitly connect the two. This is not altogether different from what Paul says. Paul too is repeatedly concerned to show that all new life in the community grows out of the gift of God; John emphasizes the point in an impressive if almost frighteningly one-sided way. Paul tends to favor the notion that such knowledge of Christ must be expressed in every department of human life, which makes it easier for him to feel that when someone outside, someone not yet committed to faith, cannot find the way to Jesus, this signals something wrong in the believing community; John on the other hand is so conscious of the miracle of faith that he is not in the least surprised that the world cannot comprehend it.

John lives in a community and shapes this community in splendid isolation from the world. The community intensifies its common life of brotherly love all the more as it listens to the Spirit of God and is deaf to all else. In this way it tries to bear witness to the world. This leads, so far as we can tell, to a communal organization similar to that of the Quakers: there is no ordained ministry. The community relies entirely on the Holy Spirit to speak the right word through any one of its members. The Third Epistle of John in fact seems to be directed against an individual who occupies a position something like that of a clergyman today. He is determined to play the leading role in his local community and refuses the pulpit to the messengers sent by the author of the letter. The author calls himself "the elder," which probably means one of the original witnesses. Here is a defense of the absolute freedom of the Spirit over against the development of an institutionalized church.

Of course there is a strong emphasis here on the fact that the Spirit can proclaim only what they "had heard from the beginning" (3 John 1:1, 2:7, 24; 3:11). The Gospel of John had made the same point before. However much the Spirit guides the community into new paths, he always calls it back to Jesus himself and his word (pp. 104–5). Thus 1 John 4:1–6 says that the only Spirit that comes from God and is not a spirit of error is the one that maintains that Jesus "came in the flesh," that he was a real, earthly man. It should not be forgotten that there was at that time a danger of disintegration. A movement was afoot which was mainly interested in a liberation of the "Spirit." It was called gnosis (knowledge). It regarded the spirit as a heavenly spark alive in every man; true knowledge of man's divinity was thought to liberate this divine spark from all the trammels of the physical and material world. The only access to God was therefore on a "spiritual" level. So this movement took offense at the earthly Jesus, especially his passion and death, that is, his "flesh." At best it regarded him as no more than a teacher of new knowledge.

The Letters to Timothy and Titus were written to combat this same movement, which is explicitly referred to in 1 Timothy 6:20–21. For these writings the disintegration of the community was a very real danger. Hence their emphasis on a regularly ordered ministry, in contrast to 1 John. Suitable candidates are to be installed by a kind of ordination, to guarantee the handing on of the apostolic tradition unimpaired (2 Tim. 2:2). As early as 1 Corinthians 14 we find the Holy Spirit creating order in the community. It is for this purpose that the "gift of grace," given to Timothy by the laying on of the apostle's hands, must be rekindled (2 Tim. 1:6). But here too the freedom of the Spirit is not suppressed. Through the word of the prophets the Spirit must first select the candidate, who is then to be installed in a particular office through the laying on of hands and so to receive the gift of grace (1 Tim. 1:18; 4:14).

These are the two parameters of church order in the New Testament. Where the full freedom of the Spirit occupies the center of the stage, as in the Epistles of John (or as nowadays with the Quakers), the community adheres firmly to the conviction that its message today must agree with the original message of the apostle, or, as we would say now, with the New Testament. On the other hand, where the need for an ordered ministry is stressed, as in the Epistles to Timothy and Titus (or as in the contemporary Roman Catholic Church or in those Protestant churches which set great store by the ministry), it is still maintained that none can be ordained unless the Spirit himself first points in all freedom to him who is called to such an office.

THE HOLY SPIRIT AS THE ONE GIFT OF GOD: JOHN

The Spirit's Reference Back to Jesus

For John there is only one gift of the Spirit, and from that gift all else follows. The presence of the Spirit is manifested when a person comes to faith in Jesus. Of course Paul would agree that everything hinges on whether the Spirit leads an individual to faith, and by so doing puts all that person's talents to new use, making them for the first time into real gifts of the Spirit. But Paul reminds the community that all the manifold human talents and endeavors are necessary to fulfill the will of God. That is why Paul attaches such importance to the diversity of gifts, whether they lie obviously on the surface or have to be disinterred by the Spirit. John on the other hand has only one emphasis: new life is created solely where the Spirit opens people's hearts to Jesus Christ. As we read in the farewell discourses, this is the one all-important service of the Spirit, the Paraclete [RSV Counselor], which Jesus will send to his disciples after his resurrection. We must now consider these words in their context.

Already in John 7:39 it was stated that the Holy Spirit would not come until Jesus was glorified, that is, until he had returned to the Father. In the first Paraclete saying the Spirit is described as the "Spirit of truth" (as in *T. Judah* 20:5; p. 34). He "dwells" with the disciples and will be "in" them forever (John 14:17). Where the Spirit is at work, there is absolute truth, and this truth is none other than Jesus, who a little earlier had claimed: "I am the truth" (14:6). The second Paraclete saying is similar (14:26). The Spirit will "teach" the disciples and "bring to their remembrance" what Jesus himself had said to them.[10] But John is not speaking of parables of the kingdom or of the teachings of the Sermon on the Mount. He means the long discourses in which Jesus spoke about himself and his mission. In an unparalleled way John thus understands the Spirit as the activity of God disclosed to us by Jesus. Where we can no longer escape from Jesus, where he holds us in motion, where we have grown to love him because we see that he gives life its true meaning, there, according to John, the Spirit is at work, though without any earth-shaking phenomena.

The Spirit's Leading to New Shores

Of course this is not to say that nothing new ever happens and that everything remains the same. The third Paraclete saying (John 15:26–27) shows that the Spirit of truth will join the disciples in bearing witness and will give credibility to their preaching. This applies particularly to witness before a hostile world which attacks the disciples and condemns them to death, as in the saying of Jesus in Mark 13:11. They are promised the assistance of the Spirit, as in Luke 12:12, and above all his instruction (14:26). The fourth Paraclete saying (16:7-11) describes the mission of the Spirit more explicitly. He shatters the self-confidence of the world with its pretended knowledge. Sin is not just any kind of wrongdoing; it is simply and solely the world's No to Jesus. Likewise righteousness or justice is not what the world thinks it is, for the world crucified Jesus in the name of justice; genuine righteousness is found in the works of Jesus, who being exalted to the Father has now come to his own. And finally, judgment is not exactly what passes for judgment in the world with its moralistic censure; on the contrary, it consists in the fact that "the ruler of this world" (that is, everything we otherwise regard as omnipotent and absolutely essential) can no longer prevail against this Jesus-event. Thus the world is on the wrong track if it goes on believing that all sorts of other things are important, but not Jesus. This shows that Jesus as he stands accused before Pilate is himself really the accuser. And his disciples, who were accused, laughed to scorn, treated with indifference, put to silence, and condemned to death, are really the accusers in God's conflict with the world. The "teaching" which the Spirit gives is therefore not a theological system whose propositions can capture the truth; it is rather a teaching that by its perpetual challenging of every new trend shows that Jesus' way is the real solution to our problems, and his person is the very truth in the midst of a world of illusory values. Almost incredibly the fifth and last Paraclete saying (16:13) says that the Spirit will "lead us into all the truth." He does not just teach the truth about Jesus; in him the truth of Jesus himself will be disclosed. There is a great difference here. It is possible to know the whole truth about a painting, all that there is to be known. But the reality of the painting cannot be grasped like that. We grasp it only when it grips us and moves us, and something of what it expresses comes alive in our hearts. In this sense the Spirit will continue after Jesus' death to lead the community into all truth. If this is what is meant by truth, it is impossible to say once and for all who Jesus is. For who Jesus is becomes apparent only when he begins to live in the situation in which we find ourselves, and to determine all our choices. And nobody can say ahead of time just how this will turn out.

WHAT DOES THIS MEAN?

In a way John developed to its logical conclusion the train of thought begun by Paul. John has nothing further to say about striking manifestations of the Spirit. The only miracle — though the world finds it absolutely strange and incomprehensible — is the Spirit's gift of faith in Jesus as the Son sent by God. Thus John, like Paul, knows that the Spirit leads to the crucified Jesus. Only now, the cross is no longer a sign of weakness but a sign of Jesus' triumphant exaltation to the Father, which means salvation for Israel and all the nations (this has been shown in our first section on John). Like Paul, John too contrasts the Spirit with the flesh. But the flesh is no longer the basis upon which a person builds his life. Flesh is all earthly reality as it exists prior to the in-breaking of the truth of God, that is, Jesus himself and thereby heaven. The flesh therefore is no longer a temptation for the believer (this became plain in our second section). Of life in the community all we could say (in our third section) was that the Johannine community fixes its hopes entirely on the Spirit, who constantly reveals Jesus anew to the believers, and through their word reveals him to others. John would not deny that this happens with different people in different ways. But he does not mention it specifically because the only thing that matters is that the Spirit reminds the community about Jesus, makes him alive again and again, and so leads the community on its way through the ages (this is what we said in our final section).

The great contribution of the fourth evangelist, which has fascinated people in every century, is the radical concentration upon the one thing necessary: the Spirit who brings us to Jesus. In face of this all human differences disappear and this leads to a oneness in the community. All divergences among the brethren become unimportant compared with the bond of unity that ties the individual to his fellow believers, that is, his love for Jesus. Of course this too can lead to misunderstanding. Paul has used the analogy of the body in which every member needs the other because each is different and therefore plays a different role. John uses the figures of the sheep who all have the same shepherd, of the branches growing from the same vine, and of the grains on the same ear of wheat. Here in the last resort no one needs the other, but all need only him who says of himself that he is the true shepherd, the true vine, and the grain of wheat grown to a full ear. This is why once and for all the community has become the property of Jesus, and is thereby separated from the world even though it still lives in the world. Both things must be kept in view: John's profound insight into the real nature of the Spirit, who makes the reality of God become present to us in Jesus, and the limitations of John's teaching, which has little to say about the operation of the Spirit in the mundane spheres of everyday life. Both are expressed in John's view of the future: In an incomparable way he asserts that with faith in Jesus we have all that we need inasmuch as heaven has thereby come to earth. Yet here too lurks the danger that the community may forget the earth and the tasks that await it there. This is what we have to discuss next.

The Holy Spirit in the Future Consummation

THE NEW WORLD

There is little mention in the New Testament of the Spirit's role in the final consummation. According to the belief of the New Testament community, what the prophets expected would come at the End has in Jesus already been fulfilled. In the community the Spirit has already been given to all, freedom is available for all, all are once more restored to communion with God, and Jesus lives in their midst—and in each member of his body—as the risen One. This is why in the Pentecost story Luke added these words to the prophecy of Joel: "In the last days it shall be" (Acts 2:17). What happened when the Spirit came among the little group of Jesus' disciples is for Luke a sign that the "last days" have broken in. Since then nearly two thousand years have passed and the world does not seem as new as all that. Was it all just an illusion?

In Paul's opinion the new creation begins where a man lives "in Christ" (2 Cor. 5:17; p. 69). Creation, when God caused light to shine out of darkness, repeats itself whenever a person is allowed to see the glory of God in the face of Christ through the proclamation granted by the Holy Spirit (2 Cor. 4:6; p. 68). John and the author of the Epistle to Titus speak of the new creation and of the new birth or regeneration in baptism. This happens when a person through the power of the Holy Spirit begins to open himself to Jesus Christ (John 3:3–7; Titus 3:5; pp. 70–72). The new world has come wherever people really learn to live in faith and therefore in true fellowship. Hence the chief gifts of the Spirit are those which foster the common life: love, yes, and joy, peaceableness, patience, kindness, goodness, faithfulness, gentleness, self-control. Where this new world of the Spirit exists there is no more need for law (Gal. 5:22–23). Thus the Spirit integrates us into the body of Christ, into a new world where its members exist for one another and are not puffed up (1 Cor. 12:13). No church has ever succeeded on its own in making this new world a reality, something more than just so much high-faluting talk. Of course the community can never live without organization, and that means never without institution either. But the real living community is never to be equated with such an institution. Sometimes the community is more alive in one place, sometimes in another. It needs the institution as a roof to shelter it but must refuse to be imprisoned by it, even if it means jumping over the walls of its house from time to time. This ties in with what Paul perceived.

For Paul has no illusions. At the very point where he speaks with the strongest emphasis and with real enthusiasm about the work of the Spirit freeing people from every bondage and recreating them as children of God, he speaks of the old creation "groaning," of its "futility," of its inevitable "destruction" (see p. 68). The new creation of man by the Spirit is not a flight of faith into heaven or an abandonment of this imperfect world. We are not supposed to become "religious" in our thinking and no longer groan with the world's groaning or watch its futility and destruction. On the contrary, the new creation means beginning to see the world as it is, suffering with it and taking its suffering to heart. Furthermore, we now learn to see the same kind of imperfection and weakness in ourselves. We learn this lesson so well that we know we cannot pray unless the Spirit takes our stupid and wrong-headed prayers and translates them correctly for God (Rom. 8:22–27). The work of the Spirit is to make us aware of our solidarity with the world. We no longer imagine that we can set ourselves in opposition to the world, devoting ourselves entirely to religion and prayer. Paul speaks in this connection about the "first fruits of the Spirit" (v. 23). The Israelite used to bring to God the first fruits of his field as a sacrifice; by so doing he acknowledged that the whole harvest really belonged to God and was due entirely to God's goodness (Deut. 26:1–11). In the same way God gave his church the Holy Spirit as a foretaste and promise for all that was yet to come. The Spirit itself warns us to be modest in our claims. Even the most Spirit-filled community is not yet in heaven but only in a threatened, groaning, and dying world. The fulfillment will come only when God does away with all our affliction, suffering, and death. The same point is made in 2 Corinthians 1:22 and 5:5 and in Ephesians 1:13–14 with the term *guarantee*. The Spirit is as it were a down payment. He is "the Spirit of promise," of greater gifts in the future (Eph. 1:13). He must be esteemed very highly because he enkindles something of the new world of God even in this world, or as Hebrews 6:4–5 puts it, lets us taste the power of God's future. Here the Spirit acts as a liberating, reforming, and healing power in individual, social, and political life. Otherwise we would find it impossible really to believe in God's future. Yet we must not overestimate the Spirit and imagine we have already escaped this world with its temptations and sufferings. We appreciate the Spirit to the full only if we understand him as a pledge of what God still intends to do for us and the whole world.

Thus the New Testament is so insistent on the fact that Jesus is the fulfillment of all God's promises that it never links the work of the Spirit directly with the creation that is still to come, the last and final creation of a new earth under a new heaven. The

Spirit is at work in this age, the same age in which the community lives, in the old world with all its needs and sufferings. Here he is beginning to build, often in a hidden way in extreme poverty and weakness, a foretaste of a new world that is still to come. But he remains a pledge that God alone will eventually bring into being a world which he can only conceive in picture language now, a world in which he will be "all in all" (1 Cor. 15:28).

THE NEW MAN

There is only one passage where the Spirit is associated with the final consummation. In Romans 8:11 Paul writes: "If the Spirit of him who raised Jesus from the dead dwells in you, he who raised Christ Jesus from the dead will give life to your mortal bodies through his Spirit which dwells in you." Thus the Spirit binds us to a God who is, as Jesus said, "the God of the living," never a God of the dead (Mark 12:27). Once again, however, this opens up an extremely difficult question.

In those days the word "spirit" was often a designation for the natural life, the emotional and intellectual power of man (cf. pp. 40–41). Naturally, the biblical authors speak the language of their own times. When Paul for instance speaks in 1 Thessalonians 5:23 of "spirit and soul and body" he most likely means by "spirit" something approximating the human reason. Similarly, the blessing at the end of a letter, "The grace of the Lord Jesus Christ be with your spirit," means the same as "The grace of (our) Lord Jesus Christ be with you" (1 Cor. 16:23; 1 Thess. 5:28). Paul can speak equally well of being "holy in body and in spirit" (1 Cor. 7:34; Col. 2:5), of the refreshment "of his spirit" (when he met his friend Titus again, 1 Cor. 16:18), of the unrest of his "spirit" (RSV mind), or—which means the same thing—his "body" (2 Cor. 2:13; 7:5), or of the "rest" which the "spirit" (RSV mind) of Titus found with the Corinthians when they received him well (2 Cor. 7:13). He says his "mind could not rest" (2 Cor. 2:13; 7:5). Perhaps John 11:33 and 13:21 are to be understood in a similar way when they say that Jesus was "deeply moved in spirit and troubled." Yet it is not always clear whether the reference is to the spirit given to man by nature, or how spirit is to be understood.

111

Survival of "the Soul" After Death? (Luke)

In Luke 8:55, in the story of the raising of Jairus' daughter, we are told that "her spirit returned." Here the spirit is the natural force of life, returning to the dead body. In Acts 20:10 Luke writes of the young man who sat by the window while Paul was preaching such a frightfully long sermon (it went on till midnight!) that, apparently overcome by sleep, the youth fell out of the window: "His life (lit. soul) is still in him." Here life or soul means pretty much the same thing as spirit—the natural life force. When Tabitha was raised from the dead in Acts 9:40 we are told simply that she opened her eyes again. But Luke also has the word from the cross, "Father, into thy hands I commit my spirit!" (Luke 23:46). Does this not mean that the spirit is something like an immortal soul which leaves the body and can also return to it again? The notion was very widespread at that time, and most probably this is pretty much how Luke thought of it. But it must be noticed how completely inconsequential it is for Luke however we picture it: At one time he speaks of "spirit," at another of the "life" or "soul," and once he avoids any such term altogether. The most important passage is where he tells how, when the risen Lord appeared to them at Easter, the disciples thought they had only seen a "spirit." Jesus replies: "It is I myself," not "a spirit" (24:37-39). Evidently "a spirit" is not the same as "I myself" but something more like a ghost. In reality, then, what the disciples saw was the risen Jesus, not a "spirit" that survived death and appeared to them. Even supposing there were such an entity which survives the death of the body, it would not be a real "person," much less a human being, redeemed, liberated, and translated to a higher existence. Only God can cause a person to "rise again," that is, become "himself" in a new form of life, a life of complete and lasting communion with God. Yet here we have the first attempt to understand what it might mean to die and rise again.

Christ and His Life In Us (Paul)

We must now return to Paul. The real problem is, what connection is there between this earthly life and the consummation of life after the resurrection when we shall really be our true selves? Paul answers this question in two different ways.

In the first place, Paul can say it is only Christ himself who really provides the connecting link. This is what he writes to the Corinthians who felt they were already in heaven in their experiences of the Spirit. Paul has to remind them quite soberly that they are not yet risen but still thoroughly alive in this world, in the "physical" body (1 Cor. 15:44; see p. 82). Of course there is a "spiritual" or "heavenly" body as well. But we shall wear that only after the resurrection. Adam did not become a "living soul" until God breathed into him the "soul" or "breath of life" (Gen. 2:7).[11] This is what we are: living creatures endowed with a soul. If there is still more to be said about us it is only because Christ became something more than Adam. He became a "life-giving spirit," says Paul. This means that in Christ the Creator-Spirit of God became so much alive that he will some day transform us into a "spiritual body," and make us "men of heaven." Just how this will take place not even Paul can imagine. He can only say that it will be different from anything man on earth can conceive (15:35–39). Of course even in the consummation all the differences between Christ himself, the "life-giving spirit" or Creator, and his creature, now risen as a "spiritual body," remain intact. Christ and the redeemed humanity are not absorbed into one another. But all that is perishable, and with it everything that separates us from God — death, guilt, law — will then be done away (vv. 53–57). Only then will we be "ourselves" in the true sense of the word.

Now Paul knows that this "life-giving spirit," Christ, has already broken into our earthly life. That is why Paul can speak in Romans 6:5–8 of the "newness of life," which is a quite different kind of life from ours on earth, one that will lead us eventually to the future "life together" with Christ. Even in our "perishable flesh," according to 2 Corinthians 4:11, the "life of Jesus" is manifested, pointing toward that final life to which God will "raise us like Jesus" (2 Cor. 4:14). In Romans 8:11 therefore Paul declares that because the Spirit of him who raised Jesus is already dwelling in us, God will one day raise us up. But this is where the difficulties begin. Does he mean that the Spirit of God is alive in us already and will go on living when we die?

In Romans 8:16 Paul writes that "the Spirit himself," that is, God's Spirit in all his perfection and purity, bears witness to "our spirit" that we are children of God. What is "our spirit"? Is it our mind or our reason? Perhaps, but in 1 Corinthians 14:14 Paul draws a clear distinction between his "spirit" and his "mind" or reason. In speaking with tongues he says his reason is suspended while his spirit prays. This clearly means the God-given spirit in which he praises God, which is why he goes on to say that it is better to pray and to sing hymns "with the spirit" *and* "with the mind." The same distinction occurs again in Romans 8:16, following the verse in which he writes that by coming to faith in Jesus Christ we have received a "spirit of sonship" which enables us to cry, "Abba, Father." Paul distinguishes between "the Spirit himself" and "his spirit," that spirit which at his calling entered Paul's life along with Jesus Christ and in whom he now takes up and responds to God's resultant promise. What Paul calls "the Spirit himself" is God's word, directly addressed to us in every moment of need. This is one side of the Spirit's reality. But the Holy Spirit is not only an event of the moment, a wave that quickly breaks, a breeze that vanishes in a trice; the Holy Spirit also determines a man's whole life, and in a certain sense is latent in everything he experiences or does as a believer, in everything he hears or says, in every sorrow or joy he feels. Thus the Spirit becomes "his spirit." This is the other side of the reality. As the love of a person envelops the whole life of the beloved and becomes the ground on which he grows, the air he breathes, constantly stirring him with tokens of love, so the Spirit of God meets "our spirit," the spirit which was given us once and for all with Jesus. In the last analysis it is always the same Spirit of God, and it is impossible to receive any other spirit than this Spirit (2 Cor. 11:4). For it is God who calls us, and at the same time it is he who responds within us. When God spoke to Moses at the burning bush Moses approached the bush not like a scientist but as one in whom the same divine fire was already kindled.

This gives us a clue for interpreting the difficult passage in 1

Corinthians 5:3-5, which deals with a notorious evildoer who was living in sin with his father's wife. Paul seems to expect that his own apostolic verdict and that of the whole community would bring about the evildoer's death. But the important thing is that Paul expects the "spirit" of the sinner to be saved forever. There is in fact a "spirit" in man which can survive death. It can be saved for eternal life even if the man has committed a grave sin. However, this "spirit" is not the soul with which a man is endowed by nature, that soul which along with the body sins and dies. The "spirit" in question is obviously that which God himself gave the man when he became a believer, the life which began when Jesus entered into this particular human life.

Christ in Those Who are Born Again (John)

John could say that such a man is "born of God." Without actually using the term, this is what he is talking about in John 11:21-28, the story of Lazarus. Lazarus had died and was brought back to life by Jesus. Lazarus's sister Martha greeted Jesus with these words: "Lord, if you had been here, my brother would not have died." Martha is one of those "if only . . ." people: If only someone had been with me then . . . , if only I had been able to go to college . . . , if only I had been able to get married . . . . She is not without faith: "Even now I know that whatever you ask from God, God will give you"—though of course she has no precise conception of what that might be. When Jesus tells her, "Your brother will rise again," she takes this to mean what she had learned at Sunday school: "I know that he will rise again in the resurrection at the last day." She had obviously had an orthodox Pharisee for a teacher. Had it been a Sadducee she would have put on a superior smile and declared, "There is no such thing as a resurrection," or at least she would have kept quiet because no information on the subject was yet available. But now Jesus gives her an extraordinary reply: "I am the resurrection and the life." Suddenly it no longer matters so much what kind of teacher she had. It makes no difference whether she had been brought up as a believer, a nonbeliever, or an agnostic. What is at stake now is whether in this moment her life goes on apart from Jesus or whether instead she finds in him a life which is for the first time real life — in which case she has experienced what John otherwise calls being "born again by the Spirit" or "coming to faith."

Jesus then continues, "He who believes in me, though he die, yet shall he live," yes, "he shall not die eternally." For if Jesus enters a person's life in such a way that God comes alive in that person, then, as we have tried to explain earlier, the Holy Spirit enters into that earthly life as a stranger and a person receives a gift he had never had before. Then something begins that does not cease even if the person dies, body and soul. That something may seem lowly and insignificant, or splendid and impressive; no matter, it is something God has begun to build. This is the "spirit" that Paul expects will be saved (as he says in 1 Corinthians 5:5), however moribund and wasted the particular life may be. Martha grasped the point, for when Jesus asks her, "Do you believe this?" she knows that what is at stake is not just a tenet of faith or a dogma to be accepted or rejected and answers accordingly, "Yes, Lord: I believe that *you* are the Christ, the Son of God." Then she runs straight to her sister Mary and tells Mary not of her new-won personal faith — she knows Mary would not simply take her word for it and believe too — but only that "the Teacher is here and is calling for you." Martha is perfectly aware that there is only one thing to do now, and that is to call her sister to Jesus himself. Then Mary will have the opportunity to receive the gift of life herself and find for it words of her own. Thus the new life goes beyond the person herself, body and soul, because in Jesus Christ God himself has broken into this physical-spiritual being. This new life, fragile and fragmentary though it be, will live on even after the death of body and soul, until God finally brings it to its fulfillment.

Here, as in the Nicodemus discourse (pp. 70–71), John emphasizes that this new life is actually present. But he knows too that it "endures to eternal life" (John 6:17; 12:25), until a final consummation yet to come. John can say that we shall then be where he, the risen One, already is (17:24), at home in the "mansions" he has "prepared for us" (KJV 14:2–3). What we have in these verses is not geographical information about the consummation; indeed John, who stresses so much the present beginning of the life yet to be fulfilled, makes it abundantly clear that this is picture language. The naive notion that we shall ultimately live "in heaven" does not describe an actual geographical location but a new form of life in intimate communion with God, a life that is already beginning here. At present this life with God is overlaid by so much else, so endangered and fragmented, but then it will be perfect and free of tribulation. Only then will man really be "himself," as Luke says of Jesus; the "spiritual man," as Paul puts it; the man who, brought home by Christ, lives eternally where his Lord lives, to use the words of John.

The New Testament Answers to the Unanswered Questions

STRANGENESS

Even in Old Testament times people experienced the breaking in of the Spirit as something alien. Yet the question remained unanswered how the blowing of the Spirit was to be distinguished from other experiences, without either confining his operation to the past in Scripture or getting bogged down with a lot of curious psychic phenomena.

Jesus must have been a strange figure to many of his contemporaries, rather like the prophets of old. Yet so far as we know he never spoke in tongues or displayed any of the striking phenomena you might expect from someone transported by the Spirit. He never thought that the clarity of the word was incompatible with the vitality of the Spirit. The strange thing about him was the way he banked on God's presence to the very end in all that he said and did and suffered. That is why he spoke in parables. He counted on God himself to speak through them to the hearts of his hearers, telling them what this meant for them. That is why he invited tax collectors to eat with him and fishermen to follow him. He counted on God to begin his work in them, showing them what it meant to live with Jesus rather than to ignore him. That is why Jesus went to the cross. He relied on God to complete his work without knowing exactly how this would be accomplished. Jesus even trusted God when face to face with evil (cf. p. 121). Even the sparrow does not fall to the ground dead without the will of the Father in heaven; why then should one fear even the evil that leads to death? (Matt. 10:28–29). Jesus did not speculate about evil or try to explain it. "If you then who are evil, . . ." he once said to his audience, making no distinctions among them (Matt. 7:11). But he did overcome evil. The old rule of "an eye for an eye and a tooth for a tooth" (Exod. 21:24–25) is now abolished and the new rule is: "But I say to you, Love your enemies" (Matt. 5:38–44). He put that into practice when he died: "Father, forgive them; for they know not what they do" (Luke 23:34).

The New Testament community was convinced that in Jesus God himself has irrupted into the world. This conviction was so central that at first the community saw the new work of the Spirit exclusively in Jesus. Luke even tried to play down the striking phenomena—the Spirit driving Jesus into the desert or Jesus' expulsion of the demons—and to depict Jesus as the Lord who has the Spirit at his command. Again, it is Jesus who "baptizes" with the Spirit or who, after his resurrection, pours the Spirit upon the disciples to encourage them and equip them to bear witness to him. What distinguishes the Spirit of God from all other spirits is not the strange modes of his manifestation but his witness: the unambiguous word of Jesus, this strange figure who runs counter to all human plans and desires. In Paul and John it is obvious from the outset that the miracle of the Spirit, a miracle running counter to all human expectations, is that he points to Jesus, yes, to the crucified Jesus.

CREATION

When the Old Testament celebrated the work of the Spirit in creation, the question was left unanswered as to how this work was related to the special coming of the Spirit, for instance his coming to the prophets. The New Testament of course takes for granted that God and his Spirit are at work everywhere in creation. But it hardly ever mentions this work because it attaches so much importance to the new creation, which overshadows everything else. This means primarily the new world which has already arrived with Jesus, the new and liberating life into which man has been admitted and which he experiences as God's new creation, brought into being by God himself even as God made heaven and earth in the beginning. This creative process continues in the church of Jesus. The Spirit teaches the community to share the suffering of all creatures to enter the lists on their behalf against all powers of evil. Knowing as it does that God will someday complete his new creation, the community is granted courage and hope to build upon it already here and now (Rom. 8:18–28; Rev. 2–3; 14:13; 19:10; 22:6–7). When the devotees of what we call primitive religions first ask a tree for forgiveness before felling it they show a better understanding than western "Christendom" of this responsibility for God's creation.

KNOWLEDGE

The question *how* the knowledge of God is to be acquired was left open. Is the mind of man a piece of divine spirit encumbered only by the evil "flesh" all around it? Or, on the contrary, must the reason be completely silent when God's unfathomable Spirit seizes hold of a person? This is where the new insights of the New Testament community are most clearly seen.

Without mentioning the Spirit, Jesus tells the parable of the prodigal son (Luke 15:11–32) to show what happens when the Holy Spirit becomes a reality. In this parable Jesus is speaking of his Father in heaven, who appears to be an extremely anti-authoritarian father. When the younger son asks for his whole inheritance the father just hands it over to him. In Jesus' day such an act would have been even more incredible than it is for us today. Is it just weakness on the father's part? In himself you would have expected him to be something like the Lord Almighty. He could have simply refused to give the son his inheritance. Or alternatively he could have suggested an increased allowance for the short term. But the father in the parable decides to opt for love, knowing that he would lose his son if he refused to let him go, and being well aware of the dangers that lay ahead. The Father chooses the way of weakness out of love for his son.

The son leaves his father, and, once in the big city, goes from bad to worse. Again, the father could have behaved like the

Almighty. He could have gone himself and fetched him home, he could have sent a friend to the city, or reported the matter to the police. But this particular father has opted for love and therefore remains impotent. He knows he would lose his son if he forced him to come back home at this juncture. Eventually, however, things go so badly for the son that he decides on his own to go back home after all, and the father, defying oriental custom, rushes out to meet him, thus showing that he had been watching for him all the time, being with him in heart and spirit. The father does not even let the son finish his confession of sin but spoils him for very joy. He has the fatted calf killed and orders wine and music making. Now the father looks more like what we imagine God to be, the patriarch sitting at the head of the table and distributing goodies to his son and to the servants. But you cannot take still pictures of God; a movie is more appropriate, for the parable does not end here.

The elder son now appears outside and refuses to go in. Hasn't he always been obedient, and was so much fuss ever made for him? So the parable closes with the ne'er-do-well sitting inside at the table, in "heaven" as it were, while the father stands outside in the dark where he could have caught a chill. He stands out there with his rebellious child. Of course he could still play the Almighty. He could call his menservants and they would have that rebellious one inside in two minutes. But again the father knows he would lose the elder son forever if he had him brought in by force. So the father is left with nothing, nothing whatever except a heart burning with love, and a word with which he can do no more than implore.

Jesus not only told this parable — he lived it. Perhaps it was only a few weeks later when he hung on the cross, all-powerful — "Do you think that I cannot appeal to my Father, and he will at once send me more than twelve legions of angels?" (Matt. 26:53) — yet powerless because like his Father he opted once and for all for love. And love is the only thing you cannot force someone else to give you; you can only wait for it with a longing heart. That is why Jesus hangs nailed to the cross, almost unable to move, and the people below make fun of him: "Let him come down from the cross, and we will believe him" (Matt. 27:42).

This is a very strange story, telling of the impotence of the all-powerful God. It is the impotence of love, a love which cannot stop its creatures from plunging into evil ways. That is why evil is an essential part of creation. Just as a child under great pressure to love and to be good, not allowed to be naughty for a moment, would become psychologically ill, so the freedom of God's creatures is unthinkable without the freedom to do evil. God's fervent love can only keep hovering over his creature until it can get through and invite him home again. When that happens it is the work of the Holy Spirit. And the parable closes, like the life of Jesus, with the persistent presence of a love which can only implore, then wait and see whether the son will yield to persuasion. Thus the story ends with the presence of the Holy Spirit.

This presence waits for us all, just as Jesus' parable is addressed to us all. This explains why the disciples always took John the Baptist's words about a coming judge as having reference to Jesus who was to baptize all who came to him with the Spirit. Luke made a special point of this. What the prophets expected to happen at the End has now begun. All who open themselves to Jesus will receive the Spirit, and the Spirit will give them power for decision and courage to speak the word of witness.

Paul developed this idea to its logical conclusion. He can speak almost like Philo of the mysteries of God which will be revealed only to those who are of the spirit, not to those who are of the flesh. But this mystery is nothing else but the word of the crucified Jesus. If someone almost engineers his own death upon the cross, the world may indeed regard this as a stupid choice or perhaps a tragic end. But that in this life and death of Jesus the depths of the divine wisdom are to be found only God himself can show, as he raises this same Jesus from the dead and through his Spirit grants us faith. Paul does not suppose that reason, belonging as it does to the "flesh," is entirely eliminated when the Spirit of God inexplicably comes over a person. Paul never forgets that all flesh is God's good creation. The only person who is really evil is the one who sets his whole store by the flesh. When that happens the flesh gets him too in its power. But where a person refuses to give the flesh such power over him it is in no way to be despised: "For though we walk in the flesh we do not war according to the flesh" (RV 2 Cor. 10:3). But this means that man's reason, yes, perhaps even his piety and morality, are neither better nor worse, neither more helpful nor more dangerous than the stronger physical emotions, his hunger and thirst, his sexuality. The miracle of the Holy Spirit is that Jesus, the One who was crucified in weakness, liberates mankind. When man is no longer constrained to live by his money, his physical strength or sexual prowess, his learning, art, and poetry, his moral superiority and his special piety, he lives, says Paul, "according to the Spirit" or "by the Spirit" – "in the flesh" to be sure but no longer "according to the flesh." He who lives "after the Spirit" and not "after the flesh" then has the capacity for genuine fellowship, so that true community can be built. He is no longer forced to play a particular role. He does not have to be an outstanding preacher, or a man of outstanding piety, or a successful organizer. He can now stand happily on the sidelines, as an unnoticed "ear" in the body of Christ. The Spirit can come in many different ways. What really matters is whether by his coming Jesus becomes Lord. And that means whether love becomes stronger than our interest in our own perfection or imperfection.

John made this point more radically than anyone. Even more strongly than Paul, John insists like Philo that spirit and flesh have nothing in common, that life is lived either from above or from below, either with the help of God or with the help of the devil. But again, the flesh is not intrinsically evil, for the Word became flesh (1:14). Evil is only the life that is based on the flesh. And again, spirit is none other than God, opening up our heart for Jesus that we may live and die as he did. So important was this for John that according to him the only task of the Paraclete, the Spirit of truth, is to remind the disciples about Jesus, leading them into all truth, showing them what Jesus means in each new situation. In face of this all human endowments vanish, ordinary and extraordinary alike. John never mentions the speaking in tongues and healing miracles performed by the community, nor social service and talent for organization either. The spiritual talents, so-called and the natural ones as well, fade into irrelevance compared with the "anointing" of the Spirit. In the Spirit the exalted Christ speaks directly to man. All the community can do is await his word. It is even a question whether the members of the community have any more need for one another.

Thus the New Testament with all its different accents is always trying to make the same point: In the coming of the Holy Spirit, God himself is irrupting into the world of man. But God does not pass man by. God does not ignore man but accepts him just as he is, in his "flesh." The New Testament authors all agree that in Jesus a new world has begun to take shape with the Spirit as its creative power, already building the heavenly world in the midst of this earthly one. This happens wherever human hearts are opened and allowed to experience something of God's new creation which came to life in Jesus. For then all the gifts which belong to the "fleshly" side of man can be enlisted for service. We may, like Paul, lay greater stress on the importance of their distinctive contributions, but only if we dedicate them to God's service, without any regard for success, whether worldly or religious. Alternatively, we can follow John and lay more emphasis on the fact that everything else takes second place before the only thing that matters: the knowledge that Jesus is the coming of God himself. But we can do that only if we stop hindering the Spirit from witnessing to Jesus as the One who came in the flesh.

CONSUMMATION

As regards the part played by the Spirit at the end of time, it remains an open question whether there is a part of man, his soul or his spirit, which survives physical death. Nowhere in the New Testament is there any mention of the work of the Spirit in the new creation of heaven and earth. The new world is already created: it irrupted with Jesus into this world and is built through the Spirit wherever people start living with Jesus. True, the Spirit is mentioned in connection with the mystery of life after bodily death. If we ask whether the New Testament believes in the immortality of the soul or in the resurrection of those who have died both in body and in soul, the answer is clearly the latter. Yet there is the "spirit" of a man which "is saved" when the body dies (1 Cor. 5:5). Jesus is "the resurrection and the life" (John 11:25) wherever he is allowed to enter into a human life and transform it. This is the beginning of a life which does not end, a life which will still be there when a person dies, body and soul. But there is no part of man which survives death—his soul, reason, consciousness, or subconscious as opposed to flesh and bones. All that survives is what the Holy Spirit has begun to build in man. What has begun to develop during our life on earth, in fragmentary ways and always amid trial and tribulation, God will bring to fruition at the resurrection. We can call it the resurrection or transformation of the "body" because God claims man in his bodily life and by so doing enables him for the first time to become a real person. Though in his earthly life man can become a "nonperson," in eternal life God alone will decide who he is in truth, namely the new "spiritual body" (1 Cor. 15:44), that person which God has seen in him all along and into which God now finally transforms him. The continuity between earthly life and the ultimate life of the resurrection is in the last analysis God himself, who keeps alive what he made out of us and brings it to completion.

5

What Then
Is the Holy Spirit?

The Various Accents in the New Testament

John seems to have meditated more profoundly than anyone else on what the Holy Spirit is really all about. That is why John is always harping with almost frightening one-sidedness on a single theme: the Spirit gives us the ability to perceive Jesus in the word proclaimed by the disciples. The Old Testament prophets had some peculiar experiences of the Spirit of God breaking through, but for John these peculiar experiences are fulfilled and transcended by the one fact that contradicts all human reason, the fact that the Spirit leads us to see Jesus with new eyes and to discover that this is the way in which God chooses to come to us.

For Paul too the basic work of the Spirit is to open our eyes and ears for Jesus. But for Paul, Jesus is primarily the crucified and risen One. Jesus' crucifixion was the revelation of the power of God in weakness. This explains the emphasis Paul places on the fact that the Spirit incorporates man into the body of Christ, distributing his gifts in such a way that every member needs the other and nobody can suppose he possesses everything, or even that his particular gift makes him superior to everybody else. Thus the Spirit builds community and creates fellowship by freeing people from seeing themselves as the center and measure of all things. That Jesus is the risen One means that even the pious believer is not yet living where Christ lives, is not yet in heaven. The community is granted in full measure the gift of sobriety, so that it can take a realistic view of the world and its needs, and be able to share its sufferings. But because God will

sert his creation, because he will one day bring it to
on, all the woefully inadequate things we are able to do
other by way of human kindness, justice, and service,
have a purpose, despite their fragmentary character. So according to Paul the Spirit grants community, freedom, and
hope.

Luke was not given to such intensive theological reflection as
John or Paul. For the most part Luke understands the Spirit in
the Old Testament way, as a gift that does not so much create
faith as grant those who already believe the strength to do
special things, above all prophetic preaching of the word of
God. Thus Luke demonstrates more powerfully than anyone
else that a community without a strong sense of mission is not
led by the Spirit and must therefore constantly aspire to this gift
and pray for it. But the Spirit falls particularly upon those we
would never have expected to receive it, on the Gentiles who
knew nothing of what religious people had known all along.
That is why the Spirit sends Peter to these same Gentiles, the last
people Peter ever thought he would be going to. Nor did Luke
forget that mission is often successful in a quite unaggressive
community life, among people who are anything but apostles to
the nations, who simply cling to their faith regardless of all the
blandishments of false leaders and all hostility. So the accents in
the New Testament are highly varied. This means that we today
must likewise adjust our emphasis depending on the situation.

The Marks of the Holy Spirit

FIDELITY TO JESUS

What does Holy Spirit mean today? We can start by putting it
very simply: the Holy Spirit makes us receptive to Jesus. The
early church believed that, to begin with, the Holy Spirit could
be seen only in Jesus. Then the church emphasized that it was
Jesus, the risen One, who gave it the Spirit. And finally Paul and
still more John perceived that the one, all-important work of the
Spirit was to make Jesus come alive for them. Once a person
begins to understand that the way Jesus lived and died, which at
first sight is so meaningless, is what brings us to order and

restores us to communion with God—then the Holy Spirit is at work. "What no eye has seen, nor ear heard, nor the heart of man conceived . . . God has revealed to us through the Spirit . . . Christ crucified, a stumbling block to Jews and folly to Gentiles, but to those who are called, . . . the power of God and the wisdom of God" (1 Cor. 2:9–10; 1:23–24). But what exactly does this mean?

GOD BEYOND OUR CONTROL

Once again it is best to start with Jesus. He probably never said a word about the Holy Spirit. But he told parables, like the one about the father who was almighty, yet powerless in his love (pp. 119–21). Jesus invited people to eat with him or to become his disciples because all through the tension of his life and death he cherished a single hope: that through his preaching, his life, and his death the miracle of the Holy Spirit would occur and God would make his home with man once more. So the first lesson we learn from Jesus is about God's presence in the world, and that presence is the Holy Spirit. We do not have to take the initiative and agonizingly strive to bring God into the world. To put it another way: we learn to live from the gift. Perhaps we can even practice this in quite a worldly way. As we stand at the top of a mountain we may be so overcome by the beauty and vastness of nature that we catch a glimpse of the universe in all its mystery. As we listen to a musical performance we may be so entranced that we get an inkling of something far beyond the boundaries of our understanding. A poem (or it could be a painting or a musical composition) may suddenly disclose the mystery of man in such a way that it changes us into quite different people, and makes us quieter, more relaxed, more confident, or more thoughtful. Something like that happens when we learn to see Jesus with the eyes of God. Only in Jesus do we behold the very "face" of God, not just—at most—something of the work of God's hands. When that happens we stop balancing the books on a purely rational level. We stop grumbling because life is so short and comes to such a grim end, without any obvious success to show for it like a growing family of children, a nice home, an original painting or novel—or an impressive textbook in theology. And we learn from Jesus to live more openly. We notice again where God wants to give us something through the Spirit. We no longer ignore it because it does not fit in with what we had planned or hoped for. The Spirit blows where it wills . . . but no one knows when it comes or whither it goes (John 3:8).

FREEDOM

Because of all this, the Spirit confers unprecedented freedom. He can come down in a spectacular mode as he did with the prophets of old, with the speakers in tongues in the early church, or with the jailer in Philippi who, after the earthquake, fell trembling on his knees and was converted (Acts 16:25–30). The Spirit can come very quietly and almost unnoticeably from the outside and enter a person's life, as he did with all those people whose conversion we know so little about except that it made them happy and comforted them, or with all the family and servants of the jailer who were simply baptized and saved along with him (vv. 31–32). But more important by far is what Paul and John call freedom from the "flesh." Where the Spirit begins to live in us we no longer have to be models of strength, whether by the standards others customarily impose upon us or by those set up by people overzealous in their piety. All this is "flesh," especially when it preens itself on its spirituality or intelligence. "Flesh" is not necessarily bad. Paul's earnest endeavors to be perfectly obedient to God and morally superior to his contemporaries (Gal. 1:14) were certainly not bad in themselves. Yet all of that belonged to the flesh. Paul relied upon it and built his life upon it until the Spirit of God freed him from his perfectionism for a life which was ready to receive God's blessings (Phil. 3:3–7). This is exactly the freedom the Spirit gives. And so amazing is this freedom that God actually loves the person who comes along with dirty hands, the person who for the moment is still empty and anything but a hero, no less than he loves a person who can look back on a life of self-denial and self-discipline. Indeed, the moralist may be further from God than the prostitute or murderer. This is incredible, but that is how it is where the Spirit rather than the letter of the law has the last word.

Hence the Spirit is the opposite of all legalism. A missionary once reported a conversation he had with an African to whom he suggested a quite reasonable rule of life. The African agreed it would be a splendid idea if the Holy Spirit rather than the missionary would suggest it to the congregation. We are gradually learning how much harm can be done when a rule, however excellent it may be in itself, is imposed upon an African congregation by a Western missionary, before that congregation has had a few experiences of its own, both good and bad, and has been led by the Spirit to the point where it can recognize what is right for it in its own particular situation.[1] "Where the Spirit of the Lord is, there is freedom" (2 Cor. 3:17).

FELLOWSHIP

Freedom has only one limit, and that limit is set not by the letter of the law but by living human beings. The Holy Spirit is constantly adding new members to the body of Christ for interplay with all other members of this body. This is equally true for one who is called in the solitude of a monastic cell or in a prison. Even there he is living with and for all the others, even though the ties which bind them and him in the one body are known to God alone. It is the very freedom of the Holy Spirit which sets these limits. For if a man no longer has to be strong all the time, there is no need for him to be superior to others nor to be inferior in his own eyes. Then he can understand why such spectacular gifts as speaking in tongues or faith healing are not a whit greater than the unobtrusive gifts of service for others or administration. If speaking in tongues or faith healing brings new life to the community this is of benefit only so long as the community realizes (in thought and in deed) that other gifts are not one iota inferior or less spiritual in the sight of God. For example, there is the gift of the mother who secretly suffers alongside her alcoholic husband and their brood of children that get on her nerves, or the gift of a man who performs a responsible service in secular society and does a difficult job without making a show of his faith. Thus the Spirit is opposed to every kind of conformism, whether secular or spiritual, and to a purely dynamic understanding whereby the spiritual person thinks himself so important that order and institution go by the board.[2] A community with no room for exotic expressions of the Spirit like speaking in tongues and faith healing can hardly be under the guidance of the Spirit. But a pious elite which openly claims — or at least secretly thinks — that anyone without their gifts is not a proper member of the community, would not be under that guidance either. So the Spirit bridges the chasms between us.

This is true not only within the community. The gifts of the Spirit which erupt in the community and serve each member merge surprisingly in Romans 12:14-15 into the gifts which cross the boundaries between church and world. It must never be forgotten that the Spirit fell on Gentiles at the beginning, driving pious Israelites reluctantly out into the "world" (Acts 10:19−20,44). The "spiritual house," the priesthood of all believers, according to 1 Peter 2:5, 9; 2:11−3:6, consists largely of slaves and women who without saying a word invest their entire lives in the service of their non-Christian masters or husbands. Paul even suggests it is the special responsibility of the Christian community at large to be especially sensitive to the whole of creation and all its suffering (Rom. 8:18-23). The Book of Revelation sees the Spirit of God in the community's resistance to all the powers of evil. That is why the Spirit is always and necessarily creating "the fellowship of the Spirit" (2 Cor. 13:13) within the community, and not only within the community but beyond it with non-Christians, and finally even with the whole of God's creation, a fellowship that is bound to have repercussions in every sphere of life, economic, technical, social, and political. Without such concrete experiences of God's present activity it would be impossible to have faith in what he will ultimately accomplish.

GUIDANCE

But we must be careful not to allow the Spirit of God to become an all too harmless affair. John the Baptist expected the coming Judge to come upon Israel with fire and the Spirit (or storm): "Even now the axe is laid to the root of the tree . . ." (Matt. 3:10-12). When the disciples of Jesus connected this prophecy with the Holy Spirit whom they had received from

Jesus, they realized it was Jesus who wished to come and judge them, turning all values upside down. Suddenly large or small possessions amassed by decades of hard work lost their importance, as did the absolute probity achieved under a rigid moral code. What really mattered now was to go about with One who would soon be hanging on a cross and, being with him, to open their hearts to blind beggars and notorious prostitutes. This is how John describes the task of the Spirit: He will turn the world upside down and show it anew what sin, righteousness, and judgment really are (John 16:8–11). But it is not as simple as that. The Spirit is not judge of the *world* only, for that would imply that everyone experienced such a judgment only once in a lifetime at the moment of conversion. According to the Book of Acts Paul sees through what was going on in the mind of the pagan sorcerer. Peter is equally aware of what was going on in the minds of two members of the community who wanted to make a great show of their piety before God and the community (Acts 13:8 ff.; 5:1 ff.). In the Corinthian church the Spirit of God who knows the thoughts of every heart probably even brings about the physical death of a sinner (1 Cor. 5:1 ff.). And the Letters to the seven churches at the beginning of Revelation are a judgment of the Spirit apportioning to them praise or admonition. "He who has an ear, let him hear what the Spirit says to the churches"—such is the closing word of every letter (Rev. 2:7). Where the Holy Spirit lives, a person is always very flexible and open. He must always be prepared to learn something new (even if it comes from the younger generation!) and to revise old and treasured opinions (even if it means agreeing with the opposition!). Then, to be sure, he may also experience guidance in practical matters. He acquires an eye for the blessings God offers him and an ear for what God wants him to do. He learns to assess practical problems and to make decisions without doing violence to others. This again can happen in many different ways. Philip knows he must go to a certain place. Paul experiences what is probably an illness as a sign from God to change his plans (Acts 8:26, 29; 16:6). According to John 16:13 the Spirit will foretell the future so that people will know what will be necessary, not only for today and tomorrow but also for the day following, for the next stage of their lives and for generations to come. According to 1 Timothy 4:1 the Spirit does not keep us imprisoned in our own illusions; he is fully aware of the dangers which lie even in the piety of the church. John 4:1–6 makes a similar point: "The Spirit of truth . . . dwells with you, and will be in you" (John 14:17).

BEING OPEN FOR GOD AND
HIS FUTURE

We have constantly noticed the connection between the Spirit and the word in the Old Testament and even more in the New. The Spirit keeps the word from becoming a mere repetition of the past. He shows us the needs of people today and leads us to ask what new truth may spring forth from the old word today. This makes us sensitive for example to the discoveries of social analysis and new social programs even when produced by groups that have little or nothing to do with the church. Conversely, the word protects the Spirit from becoming a diffused, vague kind of power. It lays down certain unalterable guidelines for the will of God and at the same time reminds us of the limits in all human planning and know-how. If therefore the Spirit gives us the power of creativity, propelling us into the future and making the word come alive in ways hitherto undreamed-of, this too is an essential part of his work. The word, on the other hand, imparts a clarity to the Spirit, reminding us of God's will and of our own limitations, and preserving us in this way from the dangerous half-truths of utopianism.

In the New Testament the Holy Spirit is closely associated with prayer. Prayer is not just an occasional activity performed at some times more cheerfully than at others. It is not an acquired facility for speaking in a language known only to the initiated (as happens sometimes even in church, where people ought to be able to speak to God as a child speaks to his father but are impeded by the strangeness of the worship language). Prayer is an attitude to life, and an opening up of ourselves to God. Often it uses no words, but simply trusts that the Spirit of God will understand what we are trying to say. Such an attitude prepares us for the future. There is all the difference in the world between this attitude to life and sheer resignation. Of course we may feel we have made terribly little progress. But where the Spirit is at work we learn to leave the future to God, knowing it is worthwhile trying to do our best when God is there waiting for us, ready to complete our unfinished tasks. The Spirit teaches us to go forth like Abraham, to learn the lesson of hope. For the Spirit points to the future where God will solve all mysteries.

Thus the church performs two important services. First, it is a constant reminder of God's infinite love for every individual, especially for the weak and oppressed, a love which leads God to take a risk which seems improbable to human eyes. Second, the church keeps a critical eye open to see that no program, whether conservative or progressive, becomes absolutized and leads to totalitarianism. For that would destroy the individual, especially the weak and oppressed it was designed to serve.

The church is of necessity united in its basic orientation toward the goal, and at the same time is pluralistic about the specific ways which lead to that goal. In the New Testament the Spirit is not the One who brings the final consummation. No, the Spirit is the presence of God for this limited time on earth. But as a "down payment" he certainly does point toward the End.

All this is summed up by Paul in Romans 8:14–28. The real miracle is that we learn to call God "Father." We can count on One who never submits to our control. Such is the spirit of sonship that it liberates us from all enslavement, from bondage either to what we think about ourselves or to what others think about us, from all pretense and the trammels of convention. Indeed the Spirit grants that ultimate all-embracing fellowship with the whole creation in its suffering and groaning. Hence the Spirit teaches us to pray, even when words fail us. When that happens, we can open ourselves to God and his guidance. For we know that "to them that love God all things work together for good" (RV Rom. 8:28). But all this is a kind of first installment of what God will be at the final consummation.

This brings us back to what we said about Jesus at the outset. Jesus is the embodiment of the whole history of Israel in the Old Testament, with all its attempts to understand the Spirit of God. All of that now comes to fruition. Jesus' whole life, and especially his death, are nothing but a constant reckoning with God, a God whom he counts on but never has at his disposal. Hence the unprecedented freedom which enables Jesus to consort with tax collectors and prostitutes. It removes the barriers which were really there between him and them, and establishes a table fellowship which reached its most signal expression at the Last Supper. It turns out to be God's guidance that leads Jesus to the cross, contrary to all human wishes and plans. On the cross Jesus has no inhibitions; he can cry out, "Why hast thou forsaken me?" But at the same time he holds onto the Father, and prays, "My God, my God."

During his earthly ministry Jesus often spoke in his parables about the coming kingdom. He committed himself to the Father's hands when there seemed to be no future either for himself or for the whole movement he had sought to kindle. So he learned from experience that the future belongs to the One who has raised him from the dead, and made him Lord of all whom the Spirit will yet summon into his kingdom.

Notes

There is a dearth of scholarly works on the Holy Spirit. A bibliography will be found in my article in the *Theological Dictionary of the New Testament*, ed. G. Kittel and G. Friedrich, tr. G.M. Bromiley (Grand Rapids: Eerdmans, 1964–76) VI, 332–34. Jewish Pseudepigrapha, not found in the Bible, are accessible in *Apocrypha and Pseudepigrapha*, ed. R.H. Charles; 2 vols (Oxford: Clarendon, 1913). Christian apocryphal writings are published in *New Testament Apocrypha*, ed. E. Hennecke, revised by W. Schneemelcher; tr. R. McL. Wilson, 2 vols (Philadelphia: Westminster, 1963–65). For the Qumran writings see T.H. Gaster, *The Dead Sea Scriptures* (Garden City: Anchor, 1976). The writings of Philo of Alexandria are available in the Loeb Classical Library, 12 vols (London: Heinemann, 1929–53). Josephus, *Antiquities* and *Jewish War* are translated in the same Library, 9 vols (Cambridge, Mass.: Harvard University Press, 1926–65). Rabbinic materials in the present book are cited from H.L. Strack and P. Billerbeck, *Kommentar zum Neuen Testament aus Talmud und Midrasch*, vols I–V (Munich: Beck, 1922–56) (cited as Strack-Billerbeck). *RGG* stands for the lexicon, *Die Religion in Geschichte und Gegenwart*, 3rd ed. (Tübingen: Mohr, 1957–65). J.V. Taylor, *The Go-Between God: The Holy Spirit and the Christian Mission* (London: SCM, 1974) is a popular and stimulating work (cited as Taylor). Written in a more scholarly-technical vein are: W.D. Hauschild, *Gottes Geist und der Mensch* (Munich, 1972) (cited as Hauschild); W. Kasper and G. Sauter, *Kirche—Ort des Geistes* (Freiburg, 1976) (Kasper); H. Mühlen, "Das Christusereignis als Tat des Heiligen Geistes," *Mysterium salutis* 3/2 (Einsiedeln, 1969), 513–44 (cited as Mühlen); and *Erfahrung und Theologie des Heiligen Geistes*, ed. C. Heitmann and H. Mühlen (Kösel, 1974) (cited as Heitmann and Mühlen).

Chapter 1. What Is the Holy Spirit?

1. M. Schirmer, *Gesangbuch für die evangelisch-reformierte Kirche der Deutschen Schweiz*, (1891) 249, 7.

2. IV 26, 2-K. Mirbt, *Quellen zur Geschichte des Papsttums und des römischen Katholizismus* (Tübingen, 1924) no 43. Cf. the Second Vatican Council (Church no 21) in Mühlen, 537.

3. Hippolytus, *Haereses,* Foreword-Mirbt 62. From the fourth century onward the opinion becomes increasingly common that the full possession of the Spirit was to be found exclusively in the monasteries, where property, marriage, and independence were renounced (Hauschild, 119–127, 284–291).

4. Council of Trent, 23rd session, chap. 3 and chap. 4, cant. 4; ET *Sessions and Decrees of the Council of Trent. Original Text and Translation,* H.J. Schroeder, O.P. (St. Louis, Mo.: Herder, 1941) 162, 163.

5. Jean Calvin, *Institutes of the Christian Religion,* ET John Allen (Philadelphia: Presbyterian Board of Christian Education, 1946), 89–90.

6. "Second Helvetic Confession 1566," *Reformed Confessions of the 16th Century,* ed. A.C. Cochrane (Philadelphia: Westminster, 1956) 13, 257–58; 21, 284.

7. H. Heppe, *Die Dogmatik der evangelisch-reformierten Kirche* (Neukirchen, 1935), 18, 24, 33, 23.

8. K. Aland, *RGG* 4, 1117–18.

9. G. Kretschmar, "Ein Beitrag zur Frage nach dem Ursprung frühchristlicher Askese," *ZTK* 61 (1964), 33–34.

10. "The Apocalypse of Peter," *The Nag Hammadi Library in English,* James M. Robinson, Director (San Francisco: Harper & Row, 1977), 339–45.

11. H. Grundmann, *RGG* 3, 799; Kasper, 19–20, who demonstrates Joachim's influence through Württemberg pietism to Marxist Utopianism.

12. G. Franz, *RGG* 4, 1183–84.

13. W. Rahe, *RGG* 4, 1178.

14. W. Zeller, *RGG* 6, 1560–61.

15. H. Bornkamm, *RGG* 1, 1340–42.

16. O. Eggenberger, *RGG* 4, 1138–41.

Chapter 2. The Witness of the Old Testament

1. J. Köberle, *Natur und Geist nach der Auffassung des Alten Testaments* (Munich, 1901), 210. On the whole topic of chapter 2 see H. H. Schmid, "Ekstatische und charismatische Geistwirkungen im AT," Heitmann and Mühlen, 83–100.

2. Taylor, 74.

3. Alongside this the word also denotes the wind as a figure for emptiness: The [false] prophets will become wind; the word is not in them (Jer 5:13; cf. Job 16:3; Hos 8:7; Mic 2:11; Eccl 1:17; 2:26).

4. Exod 6:9; Num 5:14; 1 Sam 1:15; Hos 4:12; 5:4; Isa 19:14.

5. In Gen 2:7 man becomes "a living soul" (RV). It is possible to speak of "sixteen souls" (Gen 46:18). Gen 27:25 reads: "I will eat . . . that my soul may bless thee" (RV). In the same way Lev 13:18 reads in the literal translation of RV: "and when the flesh hath in the skin thereof a boil . . ."; Eccl 4:5: "The fool . . . eats his own flesh" [i.e., himself]; 5:6: "Suffer not thy mouth to cause thy flesh [i.e., thyself] to sin" (RV); cf. also Ps 16:9: "Therefore my heart is glad, and my glory rejoices: My flesh also shall dwell in safety" (RV).

6. The spirit can be vexed (1 Kgs 21:5), or filled with guile (Ps 32:2) or confusion (Isa 19:14). The false prophets follow "their own spirit." They prophesy when "they have seen nothing" (Ezek 13:3). Job 20:3 speaks of the spirit that seeks to know more than God knows [following the author; the Hebrew and all English versions are different. Tr.]. Num 14:24 (text uncertain) says that Caleb has a "different spirit" from the rest of the people who murmured against God.

7. Cf. Job 4:9: "By the breath of God they (the ungodly) perish and by the blast of his anger they are consumed."

8. The Jewish savants connected the two passages with the gift of earthly life and with the resurrection: Gen r 14, 8, TDNT 9, 662. Cf. J. Horst, TDNT 4, 559; E. Sjöberg, 6, 380.

Chapter 3. The Spirit in Intertestamental Judaism

1. Strack-Billerbeck 1,127.

2. That is connected with the Greek idea that the "demons" are good, half-divine beings, to be identified with the souls of righteous men who after death ascended to heaven. Philo and other writers identify them with the angels of the Bible; Plutarch, *Concerning the Face which Appears in the Orb of the Moon* (Loeb vol. 12), 10; Philo, *On the Giants* 6.16; *On Dreams* 1. 140–41.

3. In a Phoenician creation narrative it is called "spirit," i.e., "dark and spirit-like air" that hovers over chaos and is the origin of all beings (Eusebius, *Preparatio evangelica* 1. 10. 1 [333b]).

4. Strack-Billerbeck 3,678.

5. E. Sjöberg, TDNT 6, 377.

6. E. Best, "The Use and Non-Use of Pneu   Jesus," *NovT* 3 (1959), 218–25.

7. Or should it be translated: "In wisdom   it . . ."?

8. E. Sjöberg, TDNT 6, 377–78, 385; G. H

9. *Ibid.*, 378–79; cf. also 1 *Enoch* 91:10, 9   nius, *Haer* 64, 70, 6.

Chapter 4. The Holy Spirit in the New Tes

1. I have tried to develop the point in detail in my *Jesus* (tr. David E. Green [Richmond: Knox, 1971]), 11–22.

2. Taylor, 92.

3. He does not wish "to be seen but to be a seeing eye of grace in us" (H.U. Balthasar in Mühlen, 514).

4. Cf. the parallels: Luke 1:5/27 (name and origin of spouse); 1:11/26 (the angel Gabriel); 1:12–13/28–29 (fear and promise); 1:15/32 ("be great"); 1:15–17/32–35 (Spirit and power); 1:18–20/34–37 (objection and sign); 1:21–22/38 (dumbness/assent).

5. Cf. pp. 51–52, 53–56, and see further Mühlen, 519.

6. Hauschild, 55–65; cf. pp. 12 ff. Speaking with tongues hardly seems to have occurred from the earliest days until the beginning of the present century. It would be better perhaps to speak of the "language of the Spirit," since "speaking with tongues" is a loaded term. What is meant is uninhibited speech which has lost all contact with rational thought. But reason is not simply suspended, nor is "the phenomenon the product of subjective emotion; it is a living expression of the Spirit" (1 Cor 14:14–16:27–33). Cf. pp. 90–92.

7. That is admittedly an exception (Mühlen 526–27).

8. Acts 8:39 is the only reference to the Spirit which "caught up" Philip. But the original reading is perhaps preserved in a textual witness which reads: "The Holy Spirit fell upon the eunuch (immediately after his baptism; in every other instance this is what happened). The angel of the Lord however bore Philip away."

9. Paul actually explains that for others all it can be at the very most is a sign of judgment by putting them off without attracting them to faith (14:21–22). Luther saw how the power of the Spirit can work even in the church's weakness. "The church is invisible, the saints are unknown" (Sauter 63; cf. 69–70).

10. Here the parameters are drawn on both sides. On the one side the Spirit is not only reminder and representation of the past, but also creative power, causing something new to come into being (see the next section and Sauter, 85). On the other hand the church is not a kind of "continuation of the life of Christ" or "extension of the incarnation" (Mühlen, 525, 533), because at his resurrection Jesus left our earthly time and returned to the Father; now he is present through the Spirit in the word of his witnesses (ibid., 533–44).

11. On the controversy over this passage in the Church Fathers and in Gnosticism cf. Hauschild, 256–72; see further note 8, Chap. 2 above.

Chapter 5. What Then Is the Holy Spirit?

1. Taylor, 164.

2. Sauter, 70–84, also Kasper, 37–38.